DAUGHTER OF NEPTUNE
...found at sea

By
Theresa Wisner

Sam's Creek Press

Theresa Wisner/Sam's Creek Press
www.daughterofneptune.com

Author's note: This book is memoir. It reflects the author's present recollections of experiences. Some names and characteristics have been changed, some events have been compressed, and some dialogue has been recreated.
Cover Design by Dissect Design

Daughter of Neptune/Theresa Wisner — 1st edition
ISBN: 978-0-578-45218-0

*This book is dedicated to the generations to come -
may each be better than the one before.*

Acknowledgements:
I'd like to thank my critique group, Dorothy Black Crow, Susan Clayton-Goldner, Susan Domingos, Susan Amanda Kelly, Patsy Lally, Martha Miller, Bob Olds, Martha Ragland, Marjorie Reynolds, Lois Rosen, Jane Sutherland, Lori Tobias, and Angelique Little for their help with critiques and editing. To Clivve Ricardo Lunn for being such a good sport while Susan Kelly and I took over their house with writerly duties. I'd like to especially thank my husband and love of my life, Rich Wisner, who read and edited, supported and loved me throughout. Mostly, I'd like to thank my mother who, although she doesn't appear much in this work, raised me with all the love she had, and taught me to be a fierce woman.

CHAPTER ONE

Long Island, New York

I smell the salt. It's carried on the breath of the earth here, and in the mist that hangs in the air. It clings to the inside of my nose and it tickles and is tangy, all at once. On my skin, a damp coating of fine crystals. I lick my lips, and taste the sea.

It was a two-hour drive to Montauk Point with my three older brothers in the back seat of the family station wagon. My little sister and baby James slept with my nine-year-old self in the way-way back. Now, like ducklings, we troop behind our parents down the docks to the white boat with *Cricket II* painted boldly in black across the white transom. Forty feet long, it's bigger than any boat I've ever been on.

There's the mate, Brian, on the main deck, waiting by wooden steps to help us board. Two steps up, grab the stainless steel railing, jump onto the deck, and move out of the way for the next kid. It's only Mom and Dad and we kids with Captain Mundas and Brian. We'll be angling for blue shark because we're little, and blues are smaller.

He's a performer, this skipper. His right sock is green, and his left one, red. I think maybe Christmas, as he pulls his khakis up past his shoes to show us his dressed-up ankles. He reaches to the deepest part of his lungs to heave words out in a voice that's riddled with the sound of an outgoing tide tugging pebbles from the beach. "Port and Starboard!" he yells. He sees the confusion in our faces and bends, palms moved to his thighs, fingers splayed inward. He's eye level with Mike, the tallest of us. The shark tooth on his necklace dangles as he pivots his head to include each of us, in turn. He backs off on his volume. "Port — that's left. Starboard's right on a boat. Know how I remember? Port has four letters, so does left. Starboard has... well more letters, so does right. I know all that . . . but my socks here?" He tugs up on his pant legs, "They're my backups in a pinch."

My feet are welded to the deck as Mundus sweeps himself

across the deck, on to other business. Awe.

We untie the boat and ride out to the shark grounds. Dad calls, "Let's head up to the flying bridge." He and the boys climb to the deck that's up top, and gather around the steering wheel with Captain Frank. I don't like heights, but I want to be with them. I scale the steps of the metal ladder, stopping halfway. My ears get a funny feeling and I have to close my eyes. Don't look down. Just don't look down.

Two more steps and I poke my head over the edge. I pull a breath into my lungs.

Dad sees me. "Go down to your mom."

"But I want to be up here."

"You'll just be in the way," and he turns to look forward.

"I don't want to be with them. I want to be up here. With you."

But the wind carries my voice the other way.

If I were a boy, he'd let me stay.

I join Mom with my sister and littlest brother in the cabin. I love Mom, but I see her all day, every day. She's always doing something boring, like cooking or cleaning. Right now, she's leaning over a sleeping James.

Margaret's sitting at the table, dressed in red pants, a red and white striped shirt, and matching red sweater. Black boat shoes finish her outfit. Her shiny hair is cut into what Mom calls a pageboy.

I'm wearing a blue, V-necked sweater. My hair is tangled. Mom started to comb it this morning but I squirmed too much, so she gave up. It used to be longer, but I got bubble gum in it last week. Mom used Scotch tape as a guide to create this bob with bangs.

She stands up and sees me. "I thought you were up with your dad?"

"He told me to come down here." I look toward the deck as my heart plunges with the shame of not being good enough. Not being big enough. And especially not being boy enough.

We motor eastward for maybe an hour before arriving at the fishing grounds. Brian grabs a bucket of stinky bait from a cooler on the deck. He takes it to the stern and tips it. The guts plop as they hit the surface, then sink. Pieces resurface and make a greasy trail beside the wake of the boat. Called chumming, it's supposed to get the attention of sharks. I don't go near it, but the smell trips over the wafting diesel, and I gag.

Along the sides and stern of the boat are fishing poles held in place by metal braces. Brian's already got those ready with line and hooks. Near them are wooden clubs with large, metal hooks attached to one end. Gaffs, he calls them. "Stay away from them," he says.

Brian's got tattoos on his arms. Mermaids. Green and blue, with a dash of red. Dad's got tattoos, but not on his arms. I see them sometimes when Mom gives him a shot in his butt for his diabetes. Pig on one cheek, chicken on the other. "Never drown at sea," he says. "Pigs and chickens don't like water. They'll surface as fast as they can, bringing a sailor up with them."

While Brian baits the two hooks at the stern, we kids circle up around Dad for directions. I'm back in the midst of my brothers and the sun is warming me from the outside in. Dad's taken his shirt off and his lightly freckled biceps radiate white under the sun. His instructions are simple. "Pay attention. Follow orders. Don't touch anything without asking. Don't let a shark drag you in."

Bolted to the middle of the deck is a chair dressed up in blue Naugahyde with worn white piping. Taking turns of fifteen minutes each, we occupy the chair by age, oldest first. Dad, with his flattop hair cut and his belly hanging out over the top of his beige khakis, stands alongside it, helping each of us get ready to fish.

When it's my turn in that chair, it's heaven; when one of my five siblings is in that chair, it's agony. Five of every six minutes is spent waiting. Wanting. Not getting my heart's one desire — the undivided attention of my dad.

When I'm in that chair, my dad leaning over me, cigar sticking out the corner of his mouth, I look out over that ocean and a calm cascades over me. There's a big, dark and dangerous ocean out there, but here, in the wake of my dad's Old Spice, I'm safe. There's something magical about the water that changes him.

He's happy and carefree. Here, he has all the time in the world.

A leather belt is attached to my waist. It clings to my hips at the sides and settles against the bottom of my belly. A rigid leather cup above my crotch and below my navel is ready to hold the butt of the rod in place. Against the small of my back, the leather extends out, creating a grab strap so someone can snatch me before a shark can pull me in.

The thing I've been waiting for happens — the tug of a line. FISH ON!

Every muscle in my body becomes a python, ready to strike. My hands are clamps on the armrests, preparing for the fight of my life. Can I do this? Am I strong enough? Will it pull me in?

Dad and Brian reach the pole at the same time. The engine shifts down a notch. The mate defers to Dad, and Dad lifts the butt of the pole out of its holder with his left hand, and grabs the reel with his right, unlocking it. He moves toward the center of the boat, slowly letting out line. His thumb presses against the spool, keeping strict control. He's making sure the shark has enough room to move, but not enough to swim too far from the boat. I'm sitting in that blue chair, the piping denting the undersides of my knees. My toes dangle two feet above the deck. Dad places the pole in my hands and its butt in the leather contraption at my crotch, gently guiding my right hand over to the handle of the reel, my left to the cork grip below it. His hands wrap around mine as he helps me pay the line out slowly. Little girl hands inside daddy hands.

The monofilament vibrates with an electric noise, quivering back and forth in the hot Atlantic sun. My god, that fish is strong! But me and my dad? We're stronger. Together we fight, and the world around me vanishes.

My arms are tired and my fingers are frozen to the rod from gripping so tight. But the shark wears down, and we reel it in. Up to the stern we bring it, and there's Brian again. Gaff in his right hand, he uses his gloved left to wrap the twine-thick line once around his fist. Up comes the gaff, over his head, then down with a thunk as it contacts the skull of the shark. His arm comes back halfway then he sideswipes it again, this time digging the hook of the gaff into the shark's flesh. Dragging it, he moves to the port side of the boat, me dogging him the entire way. I wanna see! I wanna see! I catch glimpses of the animal from behind, but I want to see the whole thing. It's my catch. My shark.

Brian lands it, then wraps a rope around the beast's tail, using a pulley to hoist it up.

The shark is hanging upside down. Its tail is higher than the mate's head, and its nose reaches almost to the deck. Brian ties the line off on a metal cleat outside the boat's house. It's an area that's easy enough to avoid, but the animal is a Siren. The mate catches my brothers and me eyeing the creature and warns us: "That monster may look dead, but sharks live a real long time. Even hung upside-down like that, he can take your arm off." We back up.

Fifteen minutes later, I'm sure he's good and dead. The shark's stomach is hanging, inside out, from his mouth. You'd think there'd be blood, but there's just this beige bag with veins running through it that spills out between rows of fangs. My brothers and I re-approach. I want to touch his skin. It looks so silky smooth, but I've heard it feels like sandpaper. I can't resist. I inch closer.

That devil whips itself up toward me and snaps, coming within inches of my face. Frozen in place, I scream.

Brian makes it to me first and grabs me under my armpits, swinging me out of the way. Dad is right behind him, his forehead scrunched down, his cigar clenched between his teeth. Brian sets me down and Dad yanks the cigar from his mouth with his thumb and forefinger. "You were told to stay away from that shark! What the hell were you doing? Huh? Huh? Answer me!"

"I – I – I thought he was dead," I whisper. My chin hangs down to my chest.

He hisses, "Never, NEVER do that again!" And he turns and walks back to the fishing chair, now filled with my little brother.

I turn and glare at the animal that has caused my troubles. His stomach is still flopping from his mouth, but now it's hanging on by a few strings of white stuff. He's bitten it almost entirely off. Still, he's alive, hanging upside down in the burning sun. I know he's alive because he's shivering.

CHAPTER TWO

Newport, Oregon

Captain Phil and I meet while I'm a nineteen-year-old waitress at the Abbey Galley on the bay front. Every morning that Phil's boat's in port, he and his fellow captains come in for gossip. They sit at two tables pushed into one, their bums settled on black, faux leather chairs. They drink pot after pot of coffee, telling stories and talking boats and fish. I listen as I serve a plate of pancakes here, bacon and eggs there. I linger as I refill their cups. Their talk isn't glamorous or even adventurous. It's about the price per pound for albacore along Oregon's coast, or which color jig is most enchanting to the fish this week. I comprehend every word, but there's something I'm missing. They speak in the language my dad uses with my brothers; all I can do is listen, and pretend I understand. Like a joke where everyone's laughing, but I miss the punch line.

It must be a guy thing. A few weeks ago, Dad came into the restaurant for a hello before he took his own boat out sport fishing. I introduced him to the gents and they sat around talking with him for even longer than their usual hour. They made that instant bond forged when the word fish is spoken to a kindred fisherman. Dad tells them I can fish. That I've caught shark and trout. That I know my way around a boat. Maybe he was proud of me. This pushed my chin up and my shoulders back.

Anyway, Phil's in his thirties, maybe forties, and he must be Scandinavian. His hair's cropped too close to tell what color it is, but it must match the red beard that covers the bottom third of his face. From afar, his brimmed cap hides the top third. His nose sits like a button, in-between. He's six feet tall, give or take a few inches. When he comes into the restaurant, he takes his hat off, dipping his head slightly as if he's hiding his height. Phil wears a set of coveralls, like my dad's. His boat is named Valhalla II, which pretty much seals his nationality.

This morning, Turtle, who owns another troller, catches me as

I refill his coffee. "Hey Red –– hows 'bout some toast? Rye."

Before he can add the words he says every morning, I reply. "And make sure it's toasted. Dark. And my hair's not red – it's strawberry blond."

"Same thing."

Can a person grunt through their nasal passages? I'm pretty sure I can. But I smile on my insides as I walk to the kitchen.

Phil comes in, later than usual. His deckhand needs to take a couple of weeks off, so he had some extra work to do on the boat. He's on edge because the fish are biting and he promised his wife he wouldn't go out alone. I walk up to the table with Turtle's toast, and Phil turns to me. "Hey! Wanna go fishing?"

There is no space between his question and my answer. "Sure!"

By the look of him, he doesn't expect a yes. Maybe he wasn't serious. And was I? What was I thinking, saying yes to such a thing?

But Phil recovers from his apparent surprise. "Uh, great! Can you get time off?"

Maybe he's thinking he'll call my bluff of calling his bluff. "I'll check."

What have I done? What did I just agree to? My brothers fish, not me. But something in my spine straightens me, and something like goose bumps grazes my guts.

My boss is working in the kitchen, and I hurry back to let her know I have an offer to go fishing. "Can I go? Will you be okay without me?"

Yvonne, a southern gentlewoman who, as the saying goes, wouldn't say shit with a mouth full of it, responds. "Absolutely, darlin'. Dawn's always looking for work - I'll give her a call. Just so you're back by Labor Day." As if maybe I'm off to play in the sandbox.

Fishing. I'm going fishing. And not with my dad or my brothers. Someone asked me for my sake, not because he had to. Phil thinks I'm fine. And I am. I can do this. My brothers do it, so I can do it. I'm going to go fishing and catch lots of fish. They'll see. So what if the last time I was on the ocean was around eight years ago? So what if I've never spent a night at sea?

I can't wait to get home and tell Dad. He likes Phil, and I know mom will go along with whatever he says. They'll trust I'll be safe with him. Not that they'll say anything. I'm an adult. Not old enough to drink legally, but still an adult.

Mom's at work, and Dad's home in the garden trying to stop the unstoppable morning glories. I crouch beside him and smell the dirt that's been heaved up from the earth on the roots of the vines. It's musty, like a swamp on a spring day when the skunk cabbage blooms.

"Hi, Sha." Dad's the only one who still uses the name my brothers used when we were kids.

"Hi, Poppolo. How's it going?"

"Damned blackberries and morning glories."

Almost on top of his last word I say, "I got a job on the Valhalla today." I say it like it's the least important thing in the world, though I'm crawling with anticipation.

"Yeah? How'd that happen?"

"Well, Phil's deckhand took time off. It was a spur of the moment thing."

"That's great. What are you fishing for?"

"Tuna."

He gets up from his weeding. "I could use a glass of iced tea."

Dad never stops what he's doing to talk with me. Beaming at this acknowledgment, I follow him into the house. He opens the refrigerator and we're quiet as he pours; the familiar sound of liquid transferring from pitcher to glass plugs the silence. He sits at the head of the kitchen table in his heavy wooden captain's chair, while I sit in a smaller version of the same chair on his right. The table is big enough to comfortably seat all eight of us. I've heard him talk to my brothers about fishing at this very table. And here we are, just the two of us.

"You know, I was in the Merchant Marine once, a long time ago. Before I met your mother."

I don't know this. But there's a lot I don't know about him. In fact, I know almost nothing of my dad, other than the stories he tells again and again about shark fishing.

"Seattle, San Francisco, Shanghai... really got to see the world." He trails off. I want to bring him back. I want to know who he was, who he is. The pendulum of the cuckoo clock ticks in the background.

"You were on a ship in Korea, too, weren't you?"

"A few years on a troop transport in the Army," he says as he almost returns to me.

"Pound for pound," he says, "tuna are the strongest fish in the ocean. They sure do put up a fight. I love tuna fishing — blue fin, bonito. But albacore are the best."

Dad's love of fishing is evident to anyone who comes to the house. Mounted on the walls are taxidermed trophies of his conquests. There's this one that's the head of a great white shark, mounted as if it's coming through the wall, jaws open and ferocious. That's Dad's favorite. My favorite is a sailfish, even though the glass eye that follows me everywhere is creepy. But the rest of that fish? Silvery-white on the bottom of its body, ebony with white spots on top. Its black tail is affixed like a boomerang.

And its sail! Harp-shaped cobalt blue with onyx spots, some of them crisply edged, others fuzzily mottled. It transforms pretty to exquisitely exotic. The black bill extends a couple of feet past its mouth, transmuting the beautiful to deadly.

I prod him with questions to keep him talking. Even a sixteenth of an inch of silence will have him rejoining the morning glories. The topic doesn't stray from fishing. I'm lounging in a feeling of closeness to this man who has been so distant. I've craved his affection or his pride, but any emotional response has been limited to anger. Now, here we are, and I don't want this moment to end.

I know the answer, but ask anyway, "Where's your favorite place to fish?"

"Now that's a tough one." He pretends to consider. "Zihuatanejo or the Bahamas for weather, but for fishing? Montauk Point, fishing for great whites," he says. "Hands down."

Dad's favorite topic is his time fishing with Captain Frank Mundus, the guy who became famous for inspiring the movie

Jaws.

"Caught that great white," he continues. "Too bad the deck hand shot it before getting it on board or it would have been a world record. They don't accept a fish unless it's hand-reeled. It was almost twenty feet long."

I know that his stories are almost over, and I don't have another question ready. I search my brain for something to ask. If I don't have a question in the next few sentences, he's sure to leave. Tick tock.

While jabbing at my thoughts, I miss something. I rejoin him in a story I've never heard before.

"...All we'd been catching that day was blue sharks," he says. "We'd harpooned a pilot whale and roped him up along side the boat as chum -- you know, bait. It's illegal to do that these days. Anyway, the blues were in frenzy, feeding on that whale. We'd finished fishing for the day and were hanging around, having drinks and telling fish stories. It was Frank, Harold Jarow, a couple of other guys, and me. We could hear the sharks thrashing. Then, it went quiet. The blues stopped feeding which, if there's food, they don't do. Then, the boat jerked so hard I lost my balance." Dad pauses, looking off toward the kitchen wall that I know, for him at least, isn't there.

"The boat shudders. Mundus runs out to the deck and we follow. There, in the water, is the biggest great white shark I've ever seen, before or since. The rest of us start talking excitedly about getting the poles out, but Mundus stands there. Without taking his eyes off the water, he tells us, 'No. We're not going after this one.' I've never seen Frank decide not to go after a shark. Even back then he was the world's most famous shark hunter."

He takes a sip of tea. I hold my tongue until it's obvious he thinks he's done. God, he can be irritating. "Well? Then what happened?"

"We unlashed the whale into the water and let the shark have him. They used that story in the movie. Hyped it up, but they used it."

I've never seen Jaws. I've never wanted to see a movie that portrayed the barbaric sport. I don't know why it fascinates the guys. All I remember is the terror of my 9-year-old self.

Dad and I talk more about fishing, but I'm sad about the shark, even sadder about that whale. I don't know why the whale is so disturbing; I guess they're the Bambis of the deep. I'd like to tell him I don't think he should kill things just to kill them, but I'm afraid he'll turn away if I do.

The fishing trip will last at least two weeks, and, other than Dramamine, I'm at a complete loss as to what supplies and clothing I'll need. I don't want to ask Phil because I want to start out knowing these things. I'm rusty at sea-faring lingo, but Dad reminds me that a bulkhead is a wall and a head is a bathroom. "I know that, Dad." Edgy.

My brothers use a sea-bag – a four-foot-tall, green duffel that closes at the top. It's de rigueur in the fishing world, so that's what I use.

My arm won't reach the bottom, and I haven't the experience to cuff it to make it shorter, but I stuff in a few pairs of old jeans along with a newer pair. I pack three sweatshirts –– two crummy ones that I borrow from my fisherman-brother, and one of my own. I pile a dozen t-shirts in, then socks. Lots of socks. In goes my favorite denim, snap-up jacket with no sleeves and perfect side pockets. Style.

Books. I choose *The Lion, The Witch and the Wardrobe*, by C. S. Lewis. I pack Tolkien's *The Hobbit* and *Lord of the Rings trilogy*. The bag bulges in spots, and caves in on emptiness in others. It looks like a stretched out, broken "W." It's almost full and I haven't added shampoo, conditioner, toothpaste, or my other toiletries. I have to pack a set of sheets — no way I'll trust that detail to the regular deckhand's idea of clean. It's likely he never removed the sheets from his last trip, leaving fish scales and other dregs. From my folks' linen closet, I select a yellow and green floral set; fitted bottom with matching top and pillowcase.

I'm out of bag, and no way can I close the top. Maybe I should ask dad for help. No... he'll laugh at the sheets, and I can hear him say, "too many clothes."

There's too much air, I'm sure of it. I take everything out and repack. I push with my foot and pull with my hands to reduce the space between items. It's little use. It looks like a messy tube of toothpaste; bulging here, empty there. I haven't been told how much to bring, but mariners bring a sea-bag. That's one. Out come jeans, socks and t-shirts until everything fits. My world, reduced and swallowed by a four-foot, canvas cylinder.

"All set?" It's like Dad's waiting for me at the kitchen table as I walk through with my duffel slung over my right shoulder.

"Yup. Packed and ready to go."

I stand at the back door, waiting for his next words — his recognition that there's something different about me. A signal of his acknowledgement that I've arrived, that I can be taken seriously, that I'm beyond that thing called girl.

"Did you remember long johns?"

"Got 'em."

"And the pocket knife I gave you?"

"In my bag."

"Okay, then. Have a good trip. See you in a few weeks."

Is that all he's going to say?

"Bye, Poppolo."

He showed up, I mean that's something.

Still, my excitement is muffled.

I take my gear to the boat, pausing on the dock to look at her long, soft lines — a swan in the water. White with green trim, much of her is left with a clear varnish over tight-grained wood. Her house is forward, and takes up perhaps a third of the length of the boat, leaving maybe fifteen feet for bow and twenty-five for her back deck. The forward section of the house is the wheelhouse, and above that is the flying bridge.

I step from dock to deck with a pinch of panic. What the hell am I doing? Tiny bubbles burst against the inside surface of my skin. I inhale deeply and enter the aft section of the house, into a small galley where a diesel burning stove doubles as a space heater.

Moving forward, I grip my bag tightly against my chest to keep myself from getting stuck between honey-colored, wooden cabinets. I clear them in about two feet and pass Phil's bunk on the starboard side, and the head on the port. A few feet forward of that, I lower the duffel through a hatch, then make my way down the rungs of a ladder to the engine room and forecastle, or fo'c'sle, where my quarters are. I set my bag up on the lower starboard bunk — one of four that run along each side of the boat like bunk beds. Beneath each bed are cupboards where I store my things. The unoccupied bunks are used for additional gear stowage. Gloves and hooks, line and lures, all neatly coiled or piled.

In this cranny of the boat, the odor of engine oil has assumed squatter's rights, circling with the aroma of fish and settling into every crevice, accompanied by the scent of a hundred past deckhands. Sound is muffled, as if I'm in a cave.

In the overhead of the fo'c'sle is a hatch that, when open, leads to the foredeck, bringing air and light into the sleeping quarters. It opens upward, and is propped on a notched length of wood to keep it ajar. There isn't enough room for a person to escape without a lot of trouble, though a small, determined someone could. That's not me. Although determined, I weigh in at 145.

I unpack. I remove the used sheets, tuck them forward of the gear on the opposite bunk, and put my own on. Even though it's a small space — even though it will be taken back when this trip is over — for now, it's mine.

Done with preparing my nest, I climb to the main deck, just as Phil's coming aboard.

"Bad news." He says.

"What's wrong?"

"The head's broken."

"What? Where do we go to the bathroom?"

"There's a bucket. The foredeck is private. Would you rather not take the trip?"

What would my brother do? What would Dad expect my brother to do?

"No, no. I want to go."

It'll be like camping. Without a campground.

CHAPTER THREE

Eastern Pacific Ocean

It's 4:00 on a chilly summer morning as we pass under Newport's Yaquina Bay Bridge. Phil and me, heading westward to the Pacific. He's up on the flying bridge, steering, and I'm sitting on the plywood hatch that covers the fish hold, breathing in the aromas of wood, oil, diesel and salt.

We pass by wooden loading docks that hold the weight of enormous scales and industrial cranes. Six-foot-square totes are lettered with fish buyers' names. *Bumblebee, Pacific Seafood.* We'll be docking at one of them in a few weeks, hopefully with a hold full of albacore to sell. Next to Mo's Annex, Tradewinds Charters is coming to life. "Quit Wishin' Go Fishin,' is their motto. Dad fishes with the owner, Burt, on the Misty; bet he'd like to be headed out this morning.

Mussels teem on the creosoted pilings and piers while seagulls yell good morning. "Good morning," I reply.

I stand and move toward the stern, breathing in the brackish air. The engine swallows the silence and sends a soft hum through the wooden deck to the soles of my feet, connecting me to this new world. Here I am, beginning an adventure. There's this thing that's been kept from me; the world of men. I have a chance to be an initiate. To find out why boys are brighter and stronger and just plain better than mere girls.

We cross the bar and the first swell gently lifts the hull of the boat, like the wake from a knee might raise a rubber duck in a bathtub. The air percolates salt.

Second swell — the whistle buoy sounds to warn incoming vessels of landfall. My Dramamine is working.

A downdraft of diesel joins the third swell, just at its zenith. I stand. I sit. I stand and wobble to the side rail.

On the fifth surge, I heave half of breakfast over the side. Then the other half comes up. My stomach is stuck on spin cycle, turning even after it seems like every drop of moisture has been wrung.

Phil comes down to the back deck. "Why don't you go on below? There's nothing to do but drive until we get to the grounds. I'll let you know when it's your watch." He points to a white, five-gallon bucket and smiles a kind smile.

Down in my bunk I lay, sleeping and puking air into the bucket until Phil summons me and I stumble up to the wheelhouse. For two hours I move back and forth from behind the ship's wooden wheel to the sides of the wheelhouse, then watch for blips on the radar screen while Phil sleeps. This is our schedule for two days — I lie in my bunk for ten to twelve hours, then Phil sleeps in his for two or three.

Maybe we could go in. It's not like we have to be out here or anything. Phil didn't have anyone until me.

No, you made a deal, I tell myself. Besides, going in would prove I can't do this. The boys would know I can't do it. Dad would know I can't do it.

It's almost dark when we arrive at the tuna grounds. The boat slows then stops, her pitch finding a deeper cadence.

"Am I still cooking for one?" Phil asks. I swear there's a smile on his face. The squinch of my eyes is answer enough.

He laughs. "It's too late to get the gear in the water. Let's get a good night's sleep and set the lines first thing in the morning."

The water is too deep to anchor, so when the engine is shut down we drift. In comparison to the constant sound of the motor, it's quiet. As I lay in my bunk I hear the wood settle and creak with the swell. The noise scares me. It seems like the boat must be splintering, and we're going to sink and drown. We're in the middle of the ocean, drifting. What if another boat comes and hits us?

The way I'm feeling, maybe that would be okay.

No, it's not that bad. Other people have lived through this.

Yeah, well 'other people' isn't me. I hate this place and want to go home.

Next morning, the scream of the engine wakes me. I dress and make my way unsteadily up the ladder to the main deck. Phil comes back and teaches me to set the lines out in the correct order; long ones first, short ones last so they don't catch on one another. Pretty straightforward: pick up a jig from its neatly coiled stack and throw it in.

Designed to mimic squid, jigs are made of soft rubber, and look like oversized bullets wearing hula skirts over their butt ends. They come in colors like orange and pink and vibrant green.

Psychedelic phallic symbols.

When I snarl a tuna line, I try to untangle it. Problem is, the hooks are hidden inside the lures and the monofilament catches on them. After ten minutes, the line is a rat's nest. Phil comes back, "Got a mess?"

"Yeah. I don't know what I did, but it keeps getting worse."

"Let me take a look." He takes the line from me, turns it over a few times, grabs a knife and cuts off the jig. "It's a goner. Next time, call me and we'll untangle it together." I tie another one on and launch it in the water.

Later in the afternoon, another line falls under my spell. It's been only an hour since the last tangle, and I'm embarrassed at my incompetence. It's an easy knot, I don't need help. After ten minutes however, it's not getting better, and my stomach is revolting from the intense focus on a fixed object. I think about just cutting it off to hide the evidence, but I think he'll notice the different jig. I bite my lower right lip and push the call button on the radio. "Um. I've got another tangled line."

"Be right there."

I watch as he unwinds it for me. "It's nothing you want to hurry. Look at the whole mess and start with the big, outer loops. Sometimes you have to make the loop larger before you pull the lure through. Do not bend it, and never force it." He's patient. I tell myself he doesn't notice I started to work on it without him.

I watch Phil's hands coax the snarl like a master conductor might pull flats and sharps out of a woodwind section. "If you kink the line, it's worthless. Kinks make bubbles in the water, and the fish won't bite. Next time, call me before you start to work on it." He says it like he'd said it the first time. Calm.

The lines are full of fish the next time I get a snag. I get one fish in and release the line to catch another, then bring in another line. Although I bring the closest ones in first to avoid dragging one fish across another, they're hitting the lines so fast that sometimes I'm half way in with a long line when a fish hits a short one. I drag one tuna into another and lose one of them. The lines miraculously intertwine. When I land it, it looks like a miniature bird's nest has swallowed the remaining fish's head.

Worried that I've ruined the line, I stand and look at it, wondering again whether I can hide it. My stomach has its own fish swimming around, trying desperately to escape.

Maybe I can cut it off and re-use the lure; he might not notice that.

If he catches you, it'll be worse.

Either way, he'll be disappointed. God, I hate this. Into my head comes every time I ever got into trouble. Every time I did something wrong. I was six and Dad was teaching me to play cards in the basement. It wasn't really like a basement since it had brown and gold linoleum floors and wood paneling. It held Dad's many treasures from trailers people had abandoned at work: a pool table, a ping-pong table and best of all, a pinball machine. Once, we had this shuffleboard table, but nobody liked it. We were using the pool table as a poker table, and brother Bob was there to make it more like a real game. I was learning how to play five-card stud, and it was Dad's deal. I knew that the cards with faces were good, and I was excited to be learning about all of this, and to spend time with Dad. Maybe if I played really well, I'd be able to play with him and his friends or at least not get shooed away. Dad takes cards seriously. Really seriously. He always said Uncle Arnie cheated, and that he should've been shot under the table. He said that's what they did in the old days. I didn't think Mom would let him shoot him, but it still seemed a possibility.

Dad was dealing and teaching, "If you have all one color, that's good, but not as good as a run or three of a kind, and an

Ace always beats any other one card."

I listened and watched intently. When five cards were dealt to each of us, I picked mine up to see what I had.

"Don't let us see them." Dad cued me. I held them way up close to my face, bending them. I had one face card – a black lady, one other black card and three reds. None of it made any sense to me, except I knew the lady was good.

"Now, the only time you can get rid of four cards is when you have an ace. Bob, how many for you?" My brother put three down. I looked at my cards then up at my dad. If Bob put three down, it must be safe. I put three down. I figured the Queen was a no-brainer to keep since it's a good card, and I chose the black two through a mental eenie-meenie-minie-mo.

Dad picked my discarded cards up and said, "Show me what you've got in your hand."

But he didn't want to see. He just told me not to show my hand and now he wants to see it and Bob will see it.

I pressed my cards to the table.

He considered them for seconds and laid them all together on the table in a row.

"See this seven here? That was a good card to keep. You have a nine and a five of hearts. Throw away the Queen and the two."

I obliged, but I didn't understand. I lost the game.

Second game and I was bored already, but I knew the next hand was my deal, and dealing looked exciting, so I held out. I didn't feel like choosing cards again, so I just asked them which ones wanted to stay and which wanted to go. Dad asked me if I wanted help and I said no. He put my cards to the side instead of at the bottom of the deck.

I won the game. As I dragged the stack of red, white, and blue wooden chips my way, he took my winning hand and my discarded hand. "Which ones did you keep the first round?"

His cigar smoke hovered over us, making a veil between the table and the overhead light.

I pointed. "That one and that one."

"Why?"

I bent my head to the side and grabbed a piece of ponytail and twirled it around my pointer finger. "They seemed like the right ones?"

"Yes, but why? What did they have to do with each other?"

"Nothing. They just felt right, so I kept them."

"Don't do that. You can't keep cards because they feel right. You have to count the numbers and find your possibilities."

My deal, and I knew he was mad at me, so I tried to shuffle them the best I could. Not like a kid – like a real card player. I separated the stack into two piles and bent the cards. The ones in my left hand stayed fine, but the right hand let fly everywhere. I picked them up and Dad told me to shuffle them the kid way, so I messed them up all over the pool table and stood up to collect them.

I dealt and then replaced two cards for Dad, and Bob got three. My choices remained confusing to me. There was a possible run, but I didn't like runs. So I kept my Ace and my nine – lucky nine. Dad pulled them over to the side again. In my deal, I got two more Aces.

Dad asked again why I chose them and I put my gaze on the green felt.

"What in the world am I doing trying to teach you? You can't just use a guess to decide which cards!" He threw his hand down on the table and stomped up the stairs. Bob helped me clean up the deck, but when I tried to meet his eyes, he was looking down. But I'd won, and I didn't understand why Dad was mad – I thought winning was good.

I turn and call Phil.

"Nice one," Phil jokes as he joins me. The snarl in my stomach relaxes. He removes the hook from the tuna's mouth. "Keep hauling fish. I'll tie this off and we'll come back to it when the bite's over." He returns to the wheelhouse to turn the boat back over the school. I'm confused that he's so patient. We catch fifty albacore in the best fishing we've had.

Phil rejoins me and picks up the nest, handing it to me. "See what you can do with it. Slowly. And remember, you're loosening things up first." He sits down next to me and watches.

Soon, the wad of nylon strings is as big as a basketball, and I haven't kinked the line. Pretty good.

"Let's see," he says. Phil takes it and finds the hook, then works the line through. When it's about half un-done, he hands it back. "You can get it from here." He leaves me to finish the unravelment.

With time, I learn to work with the line rather than against it, and I'm able to tease the knot apart.

The Zen of untangling monofilament.

CHAPTER FOUR

Eastern Pacific Ocean

After a week, I wake up and the queasiness is gone. Replacing it is a sense of calm, and the beginning of this idea that I belong here. I'm connected to the sea through the umbilical cord that is the Valhalla. The fish start biting, but more importantly, I'm at peace for the first time I can recall. Ever.

I grow accustomed to the quiet in the few moments before I drift off each night. The noises that once frightened me become a comfort; a lullaby sung through the heart of the wood as the boat sways me gently to sleep. These are the halcyon days of tuna fishing.

On deck, I have few thoughts other than when the line might grow taut from a fish bite, or when to move the fish from the deck to the brine solution in the hold. I'm up long before daylight and asleep well after dark. Each day is cut into pieces: Wake up. Get dressed. Set lines. Cereal. Before morning bite. Morning bite. After morning bite. Brine fish. Lunch. Maybe an afternoon bite. Brine fish. Nap, glorious nap. Back on deck for the possible stray bite. Brine fish. Dinner. Evening bite. Brine fish. Day done. Undress and crawl into my bunk and pass out until Phil fires the engine up the next morning. Start over again.

Between bites, I read or practice songs on deck, waiting for the monofilament to sing the news: "Fish On." As long as I catch them and brine them, my life is complete. I have no other responsibilities. I'm alone as Phil steers the boat from the wheelhouse, fifty feet away.

I haul tuna halfway up the transom and swing them upward in an arc and back over my shoulder to a hard landing on top of a plywood platform. Most of the time, they're flopping around. Their mouths open and close like a smoker making rapid-fire smoke rings. The sound of tuna on the deck is like this: Rest your wrist and palm on the top of a table, then tap your hand as fast as you can and pretend twenty of your friends are in the room with you, doing the same thing. Each hand is a fish. I've heard the fishermen do this in the Bay Haven, and now I know what it's all about. Dad talked about the boys being "in 'em," and now I know what he meant. I look forward to telling him my own stories, and having him listen.

I wear gloves at first, but they make me clumsy. After I lose a few fish, I take them off. My hands aren't accustomed to the bite of the lines, or to being constantly wet. They're torn and raw, and the salt water dries them out. On the inside joints of my knuckles, I have splits in my skin where the lines dig in. I unconsciously draw my hands closed in my sleep, and each morning I un-freeze them, one mangled finger at a time. When my hands are completely open, I spread them apart and curl them down into a fist, then straighten them out. They hurt. They bite. They sting. After a few mornings of this, I mention something to Phil. He looks and a frown rumples his face. He goes to the wheelhouse and returns with a square, green can. He opens it and has me dig my fingers into a Vicks Vapo Rub-smelling, yellow-tinged, Vaseline-like substance.

"Bag Balm. It's for cow udders, but it's the best medicine for this. Rub it in every night and cover your hands with clean cotton gloves. There are a few pair in the empty bunk. You should be back to new in a few days."

Christ. Bag Balm? I'm putting cow medicine on my hands? What am I, a farm girl?

The next morning however, it takes half as long to unfurl my fingers. Day two takes even less.

The fish are off the bite. Nobody's catching this morning, and the radio's silent; nobody wants to talk about not catching. On the deck, I back myself up to the cover of the hold and sit, cross-legged. With nothing better to do, I sing my own rendition of *Born To Be Wild*. Even if someone was close enough, no way they could hear me over the engine, and I know Phil's looking ahead. The gaff is my microphone and I tilt my head to the side and back as I sing-shout the lyrics. "Like a true. Nature's. Child. We were born. Born to be wild. We can climb so highhhh I never wanna diiiie. Born to be wi-i-i-i-ld. Born to be wi-i-i-i-ld." My eyes are shut tight so I can envision my audience. Mermaids, perhaps? The fish are clearly not entertained. I put the gaff down and try another song.

Still seated, I use my arms to add depth and meaning: "Y-M-C-A it's fun to stay at the Y-M-C-A-ay. They've got ev-eree thing that you need to enjoy, you can hang out with all—"

"Hey, Theresa," from the loudspeaker. I jump. "You might want to head up to the bow."

Shit. Did he hear me? Did he see my arms doing the *YMCA* thing? Am I in trouble?

I jump up and rush along the walk, past the wheelhouse.

It's chillier up here than it was on the back deck, and the taste and smell of the salt air ride the breeze created by the motion of the boat.

Phil joins me on the foredeck, then points to a spot, starboard of the bow. "Take a look."

I see a shimmer beneath the water's surface. My vision is focused on it, but it's as if I'm looking out the corner of my eye. Shadows and light veil a flash of sinewy white. Dolphins. Four of them, right in front of the boat. I see one clearly now, black and white with a slender nose. It swims up, slaps its tail against the bow of the boat, surfaces, then dives. Another chases close behind, copying the path of the one before. Each one of them follows, and then they begin their boat-waltz-slap again. Sleek creatures that sing to my heart and cause eddies of delight in my belly. They keep pace with the speed of the boat, never faltering in their beautiful dance. I lay down and cradle my belly against the wooden deck and stretch my head out beneath the bottom rail of the bow of the fishing boat, watching those dolphins play.

An hour later, the visit ends with the zing of a tuna line tightening. Fish On! I jump up and head aft as the afternoon tuna bite begins. We bring in almost three hundred albacore.

This is the day I become hooked on tuna fishing. I understand the allure it holds for Dad and my brothers. The interlude becomes the center of my search for peace on boats. The sea becomes a place of possibility, of magic. It holds the chance for change, for a new and different life.

But the alchemy goes retrograde as we close in on Labor Day weekend. The stink of fish oil and diesel has replaced the sweet brine of a summer morning, and I want to go home. Phil has other ideas.

"Fishing's good. Best so far this season."

"Glad to hear that." I wonder what that shower's gonna feel like.

"You're probably making more money than you would be waiting tables."

My instincts straighten up. He wants to keep fishing! Is he nuts?

He continues. "Maybe we can stay a few extra days. They probably won't miss you too much."

No! No! "Wow, Phil, I'd love to, but I promised Yvonne I'd be back. It's going to be hard on them if I can't make it."

"We can get a message in. Maybe they can find someone to replace you. Fishing's really good."

I'm done with this. Shit. I want a beer. I don't want to be here at all.

"I don't think so, Phil. I made a promise." I love it when a promise works in my favor.

Next day, we're heading in. I'm hauling tuna on the back deck and most of the lines have a fish on them.

The radio chatter is constant, but I've learned to ignore it – it's background noise. I can't hear what Phil says, so it's a one-sided talk. But this conversation's got my attention.

"You're leaving this bite? What, are you crazy?"

"Crckkcrcklcrkc." That's the noise of the release of the other boat's mike, then silence, meaning Phil's got his thumb pressed on the mike.

"Crckkcrcklcrkc."

"Did'ya try and get her in the sack and she wants to head in now?"

"Crckkcrcklcrkc."

What? What are they talking about? Phil would never try anything like that. And even if he did? Yuck! He's old enough to be my dad."

Damn, I want to hear both sides. I want to hear Phil tell this guy off.

But I live with the thought that he must have told him off. I'm too embarrassed to ask him about it, and I guess he's too embarrassed to tell me.

It's a cloudless morning and we have no breeze. A lightly shaded ridge appears on the eastern horizon. As we near, there's a smell. It's familiar yet foreign, all at once. It's comforting, but disconcerting. I think I'm imagining things, but I figure I'd better mention it to Phil.

Not sure how to approach it, and not wanting to feel foolish, I go to the wheelhouse and stand for a few minutes to see if maybe he's smelled it and then I'll be off the hook for imagining things or thinking something's important that isn't. Worst of all, it could be something I finally smell that I should have smelled all along.

But Phil only points out that we'll be at the dock in a couple of hours.

So I dive in. "Hey. Um. I smell something odd on the deck?"

"Is it diesel?"

"No, it's nothing mechanical."

"Is it fishy? Salty?"

"No, it's familiar, but I can't place it."

Phil leaves the wheel on autopilot and joins me on the deck. I hear him as he draws a nose full of air, "Ah." Another whiff, as if confirming. "That's land."

I've never heard of such a thing, and if Phil weren't Phil, I'd think he was pulling my leg. I inhale deeply through my nose, my eyes lightly closed. "Ah," I repeat, as if I understand. But I don't understand at all.

I continue to breathe the aroma, trying to pinpoint what it is. Then I finally catch it in my mind and heart rather than just my nose. It's been too close to me to even recognize as a scent of its own. It's earthy like the green and brown of the deep fir forests of the Pacific Northwest. I sense the slightest suggestion of shore pine needles. Maybe it's my imagination that I can pull those scents out. It could be a blur of everything mushed together in one nebulous slurry, like when it rains for the first time in a long time and there's the smell of pent-up oils springing up from a parched earth. Petrichor.

There's also an undertone of an off scent that comes and goes. Like someone at the far end of a crowd peed their pants or something. The chemicals from the paper mill at Toledo? Too far, I think. The asphalt plant? Could be. Maybe it's the exhaust from cars on Coast Highway. Whatever it is, I'd rather I couldn't smell it. Overall though, the smell is welcome as a sign of familiarity. It reminds me that I'll soon be able to get a hug. I'll sleep in my own bed, and have the shower I haven't had for two weeks. But most of all? I'll get a cold Heineken.

As we motor through the bay, fishing boats are leaving and sailboats are flexing their sails, trying to catch the exhale of a breeze. Home. We motor by the same restaurants and fish plants, and head for the dock. We'll unload the fish at the cannery tomorrow.

As we near the Valhalla's slip, I throw the orange fenders out to protect the boat. As soon as they touch the wooden planking, I grab the line and jump on the dock, as Phil had instructed me.

Seconds after my feet hit the boards, vertigo rushes over me. Unbalanced, I miss the cleat I'm aiming for. I stand upright to get my bearings, but immediately have to bend over the water to puke. I've never heard of land-sick, but it's as bad as seasick.

CHAPTER FIVE

Newport, Oregon

The following summer, I'm working as a waitress at Mo's in Newport. It's a hole-in-the-wall restaurant with a dark interior and tables made of old hatch covers painted with half an inch of clear acrylic. The floor is polished concrete, and the walls are dark wood, covered with maritime memorabilia.

After six-hour shifts of taking orders for New England style clam chowder, garlic bread and peanut butter cream pie, I join the bar crowd on Newport's bay front. I start at the Bay Haven tavern where the beer is on tap and the wine comes in cardboard covered Mylar bags.

After a few beers I move west to the Pip Tide. It's the classiest of the pair. The two-story dive has live music by pasty-faced, glitter-spackled rock-and-roll bands downstairs, Poker and Black Jack upstairs, and drug deals everywhere. The carpet smells of old beer and nicotine with an undercurrent of men's locker room. At night the combination is masked by the smell of fresh cigarette smoke and hard liquor, with a dash of man-sweat added in. Adjoining the bar is the 24-hour restaurant that recently replaced Lou's Dog House as the number one after-hours dining experience in town. I'm attracted to this place because nobody's concerned with my age – south of legal.

I like working at Mo's, and I've moved from cooking to waiting tables, a big increase in pay. Well, a drop in hourly wages, but tips more than make up for that. I love my co-workers and the head waitress, Jan. I love Mo and her granddaughter, Cindy. But being stuck inside a restaurant for the summer and gazing out on sunny days is already making my feet tweak, and it's only March. I miss the ocean, although I don't miss the seasickness. I do miss the immediacy of it — the clear connection between what I'm doing and where I am. Here, I'm feeding hungry, cranky strangers who wouldn't know if I died tomorrow. Out there, it was the water, Phil, the boat, and me. I felt alive.

During the summer months, Mo's is so busy there's almost always a line of customers spilling out the door, waiting for their turn to sit down in front of a bowl of chowder. They stand on the sidewalk outside the open garage door that offers ventilation into the overloaded dining room. I'm waiting on a group of people at the table next to this door when I look out and see a pair of fisherman's coveralls. They're out of place on the tourist-lined concrete. I look up to see Phil's smiling face, and give a surprised smile back. I finish taking the order and step outside since it's obvious he didn't come for the soup. He doesn't waste time getting to the point.

"I need a deckhand. Not for one trip. I need someone for the season."

"Gosh, Phil, I don't know anyone who's looking. Let me ask around."

"I thought maybe you'd be interested. We got along pretty good last time."

Me? Me? He wants me?

"It's supposed to be a good tuna season," he continues. "The velella velella are already showing up on the beach." He says it like an Italian song... vellavella... They're a violet-colored jellyfish with translucent sails. Their spinnakers catch the breeze and push the aimless creatures wherever the winds carry them. Sometimes they're blown onto the beaches by the millions, piling up on the sand. The rancid stench of decomposing marine life smells for blocks inland — a salty smell like a mix of seaweed and rotting fish carcass. The velella velella inhabit the same warm waters the tuna swim, and the lore is that when they blow onto the coast, the tuna will run, sometimes as few as fifty miles offshore.

What do I say? How do I respond? A pause while my heart and my head fight. Adventure or stability? Fun or security? "I don't think so, Phil. I'm going to school this fall."

"The season should be over in time for you to start the term. Or at least slowed down enough that I can handle the deck on my own."

If it's a good season, I can make a lot more money than I can waiting tables, and I'm tired of waiting tables.

"You'd need to start in a couple of weeks — like a regular deckhand. I need help painting and varnishing and setting the gear. We'd start out with salmon, then switch over to tuna when they get in close enough." Another breath. "And I'll get a portable head for you to use. You'll have to empty it, but it'll give you privacy."

I'm not able to reply because so much is going through my head. I'm already sitting in the bar, telling stories about the one that got away and the ones that didn't. I'm playing a game of pool with my dad and easily chatting about fish and the ocean.

"Regular deckhand gets 15% off the top. That's before expenses."

I know what an experienced deckhand makes, and what a green one makes. He's offering me the higher cut.

"I'd like that, Phil. I'll come down and check in with you after I'm off."

My bounce is hard to contain the rest of that day, until the afternoon draws to a close and I get closer to having to tell Jan. I want to put it off. I don't want to tell her at all. I feel like I owe her something, though I couldn't say what. I'm afraid I'll disappoint her and Mo. But I want to go fishing more than I don't want to quit. But, Jan, in her usual style, makes it easy for me, saying that if she were in my shoes, she'd do the same.

I walk down Bay Boulevard to the boat, and make final arrangements with Phil.

At home, Dad's in his easy chair, getting ready for the news programming to begin. If I don't get my own news to him quick, he'll be in TV land for at least an hour.

"Hey, Dad. Phil came in today. Asked me to come work for him this season."

"That's great, Sha. What's he fishing for?"

"He says we'll start out with salmon, and go for tuna when they're close enough. I'll do boat work for a couple of weeks before the season opens."

"That's great."

His eyes are fixed on the screen. He's gone already.
We'll talk later, I tell myself.

CHAPTER SIX

Western Iowa

G rowing up with three older brothers, it was easier to follow their example than it was to create something new. I followed my brothers wherever I could. Also, by decree of our mother, I tagged along with them most of my childhood, and into my teens. They were, in effect, my babysitters. How did they feel about the relationship? I was an unwanted mole in the middle of their boyish chins: Impossible to hide, embarrassing, and as much ignored as I was glaringly present.

Along with many other skills, my brothers taught me to jump. There was the time we were in Iowa, visiting my grandparents. We rode some borrowed bikes and pedaled to the Des Moines River. I was about eight. There was a train trestle that crossed over a deep spot in the river that made the perfect diving platform. I walked out there with them, but got scared about midway. I hesitated, then put my eyes on Patrick in front of me and made it to the diving place. Every fifth or sixth tie extended out a few feet, and the boys used them as rigid diving boards to jump into the black waters below. That water was a long way away. I figured I could run three houses down in my neighborhood and still not take up the distance that water did.

Right after they jumped, they crossed their legs at the ankles and put a thumb and forefinger over their noses so they wouldn't inhale liquid. They hit the water with a sound like a cannon charge, then sank. They'd swim to the shore and scramble up the bank, then run back onto the trestle. All afternoon. Jump, swim, scramble, run. Jump, swim, scramble, run. The hot Midwest sun burned from above, melting the tar on the trestle, which seemed to give back twice what it received. I sat on a towel on one of the railroad ties, and looked down, daydreaming about what it might be like to be in that water instead of on the trestle breathing the perfume of hot creosote. I practiced holding my breath to see if I could do it. I took a big gulp just before they'd hit to test myself. One-one-thousand, two-one-thousand, and on up to ten one thousand. Yep, I could have done it, but I never was a jumper. The boys teased me about it, but I didn't care.

Patrick and I were standing on the bridge when the whistle blew. That sound shot a bolt of electricity through me and I froze. I looked up to see the train coming around the bend on its approach to the trestle. Pat must have sensed my decision to run because he grabbed my wrist and said, "There's no time."

"I'm not jumping!"

"You'll only get halfway and the water's not deep enough there!"

I look at the train. It's on the trestle now and I see the logic in my brother's argument. But still... it's too far down. What if I belly flop? I'll drown for sure.

"I'll just move out to the edge and wait for it to pass." This is a plea, not a statement.

"Get out here. Now!" His skinny little body was bent toward me, hand held out.

I moved to the edge of the railroad tie and looked down. I knew I couldn't do it but that whistle was blowing again.

Pat said, "I'm not going without you. Push out when you jump."

Ohmygod. Why did I come here? Why didn't I just stay with Mom and Grandma? I squitched my eyes closed and smooshed my nostrils together with one hand while I hugged myself with the other. My toes clasped the tips of the ties and I used the balls of my feet to leap out from the track and into blind faith that my brother was right.

Blackness as I dropped through hot air. The dense humidity was a wet sponge on my skin, but the rest of my senses were in blackout. And I remembered — or maybe I'd practiced so many times when they jumped that I just did it. I grabbed a lungful of air before my toes hit the cool water and I sank like a jet-propelled engine. Then the downward motion stopped and I began to surface. I opened my eyes and clawed toward the light and then there was air that I could snort in and there was Pat surfacing beside me. Above, the train screamed our success and good wishes. Pat laughed and I laughed right back.

I waited for the boys on the bank of the river. They lost track of time and the sun was whispering to the horizon when they made their last ascent of the bank.

Now, at twenty, I'll follow my brothers to sea. Mike and Bob are fishing in Alaska and Pat's working on a dragger, combing the sea floor with a net for rockfish. Salmon and tuna are not so glorious or dangerous as bottom fish and crab, but I'm getting there. I'm on the low diving board, but the high dive is right next to me — in sight.

CHAPTER SEVEN

Newport, Oregon

Two weeks to the day after my conversation with Phil, I walk down the dock to the Valhalla. No, that's not true. I sashay. My stride is a precise balance of flounce and glide. I've been on these docks a hundred times before, but now they're mine. I fit like a ballerina on a stage, like Jell-O in a mold.

The smells of diesel and creosote fill my nose. The sounds of power tools and hammers against nails fight for airspace, their dissonance like a new-age jazz band in my ears. Guys are working on decks, sanding, painting, and tying gear. Some of them I know, some I don't, but I smile at each of them and say hello. They are, after all, my comrades. We are the select few who get to make our living fishing. The dream. Lots of guys would take my spot in a breath. But Phil didn't ask them, he asked me.

Two more weeks of sanding and painting and sunburns and then we're back at sea. I learn that I don't like salmon fishing. First, the trips are near-shore and short — less than ten days. That means I get sick each new trip for at least a few days. Although it's good on my weight, I don't like being sick. I've tried ginger and Dramamine, soda and crackers. This time, I even got a prescription for Scopolamine. The patch that goes behind my ear makes my mouth dry, and my brain behaves like a rotting watermelon.

Salmon's more work, too. I have to clean every fish and pack ice into each one of their bellies in the hold, ice-side down so water won't puddle inside and spoil the delicate fish.

The work is slow. Put the lines in the water and soak them for an hour or so, depending on Phil's fish sense, then bring them up. Maybe there're fish, maybe not. When we do get a fish on, there's no fight in them, at least compared to tuna. I pull the salmon up to the boat and use a long handled net to land them. They offer little protest, even after they're on board.

Salmon fishing is solitary. Boats don't share their position, and the radio is silent. The sound of it crackling with voices while we were tuna fishing was annoying, but the silence is more uncomfortable. More alone.

Day one we catch two fish. It's excruciating. I'm used to activity and exercise. If I'm going to come out here and be seasick, I want a reason. This is torture. I read. I sing. My goal for this trip is to remember all the lines to Peter, Paul and Mary's *Leavin' on a Jet Plane*. I have verse one: All my bags are packed, I'm ready to go, I'm standing here outside your door. I hate to wake you up to say goodbye...

I write. In my journal, I tell stories about Aquatel, and a girl named Dierdre who tries to kill herself, but gets swept out to sea. She's adopted by the Aquatellers, descendants of the Lost City of Atlantis. They've moved to a deeper part of the ocean to avoid the violence of humanity. Dierdre is adopted by the royal family, and she finds friends and happiness.

From time to time, dolphins are visible in the distance, but they don't get as close as they did on the last trip. I watch for whales, but none appear. I swear this will be my last trip. I can't live this way. Salmon fishing sucks. Screw the weeks of deck work. Screw the money. Screw what Dad thinks.

But Phil needs a deck hand and I'm not a quitter. The tuna will come in close soon enough, I hope.

My singing is interrupted on our fourth afternoon. "Go ahead and check the lines," Phil calls over the intercom.

I stand and press the button on the deck mike. "Will do." I'm an automaton. Lines up, lines down. I pull up empty hooks, one after another. Nothing's happening, so I'm not expecting anything. Halfway through my routine, I see a fish. Finally. I slow the hydraulics and grab the net. No gaffs here – they might damage the flesh of the salmon.

This one is enormous! I'd better call Phil before it surfaces and I lose it.

I stop the upward journey of the line and get back on the mike, "Phil, I might need help with this one."

"Be right there."

The engine slows, creating less tension between the hook and the fish, decreasing the chance of losing him. A puff of diesel slows on the air and surrounds me and I hold my breath and crinkle my nose.

Phil comes to the transom and, not wanting to take responsibility for the expensive fish, I hand him the net. He takes it and looks over the side. "That's no salmon. It's a shark. Let's bring him in."

"Bring him in? You mean, like, onto the boat?"

"Yeah. I'll show you what we do with sharks."

I turn the hydraulic lever on to bring it up the last few feet. Phil grabs the line with his leather-clad hands and draws it up to the stern. Using the gaff, he pulls the struggling shark on board. He removes the gaff and uses it to club the creature on the head a few times, knocking it out.

Its eyes are perfectly round and enclose circles of black. They look as if they might jiggle if I shake the head — like floating eyes on a cheap doll. Phil flips it on its back, revealing a long white belly. Its curved mouth is etched in black, midway back on the torpedo of a snout. Phil pulls a filet knife out of the wooden rack and deftly cuts the shark's jaw out, sawing through white flesh that doesn't bleed.

I'm not sure if it's shock or awe that I feel. There's a violence that I've never seen in Phil. Hatred. I guess I'm staring at him because he says, "You'll understand when they eat a thousand bucks of your fish."

Dad has shark jaws like this one, only bigger. Now I understood how they got there.

To bide the time, we search for rip currents — places in the water where two currents meet, collecting and trapping pockets of oily green seaweed. More prevalent than seaweed is the garbage, supplied by humans. Sometimes it comes from boats; mostly it comes from what people leave on beaches. The tide comes in and flushes it out like one big septic system.

It doesn't take long for us to find a line of floating debris. There's no visible end to the bobbing plastic. It's green, blue and orange, white and red. The pieces float around, bumping up against each other like New Yorkers at a white sale. But there's treasure floating among the trash: Japanese floats. Fishermen from across the Pacific have hand-blown them for centuries, using the floats to keep the top of their nets at the surface.

I'm scanning the water, looking for something round and floating higher than the rest of the rubbish. We search for maybe twenty minutes when I find the prize. I run to the wheelhouse and yell, "I found one! I found one!" As if one scream isn't enough. Phil drives to the spot I've pointed out while I grab the net and move to starboard. We head into the mass of waste, separating it like a comb would part a head of spaghetti-thick hair. Up close I see blue and white oil jugs, translucent milk bottles, Barbie's head. Phil's got one hand on the wheel, and his head's sticking out the wheelhouse door. The thunder of the engine reduces to a rumble as we pull alongside a moss-green Japanese float. He puts the boat in neutral, making the noise a comparative whisper. I dip the net into the water, scooping at the orb as Phil joins me. I struggle with actually catching it — it's not as easy as I'd thought. It's bulky and heavy, so I miss it a few times and then struggle to pull it toward the boat. I use the aluminum ring of the net to scooch it closer, inch by inch. At the halfway mark, I hit it just-wrong and it scoots away from me.

"Crap." Finally, I get the filled net to the side of the boat. I try to lift it up, but no way I'll get it on board. Phil laughs and holds his palms out and I drop my shoulders and hand it over. Uncle. He takes the handle and brings it up close enough that he can grab the net ring. Together we wrestle it aboard. It's over a foot in diameter and has a three-foot long beard of mussels and barnacles attached to its netting. The smell is like a mooring at low tide on a winter day.

"It's yours, if you want it," Phil says.

I look away from the treasure, toward my benefactor. "Mine? Really? You don't want it?" I answer in a half-exhausted breath.

"I have some at home and the rule is: you find it, it's yours."

"Thanks... Thanks!" My eyes rest on his for another second before I grab a knife to cut the shells off.

"Soak it in bleach when you get home and maybe you can keep

that netting," he suggests.

"Yeah. Will do," focused on my treasure.

The find changes my attitude. We still aren't catching much, but hope is woven into the horizon. The float is my rainbow, and I know the fish are going to start biting.

To amuse myself while waiting for the magic to happen, I look at the inside surface of the lens of my eyeglasses and watch the reflections of my eyes and eyelashes show up when the sun hits the glass right. I blink and observe. Around my eyes, fine wrinkles are beginning to form, crows dancing their first jig. Nothing is boring now. Nothing is beyond notice. I'm hyper-alert to my surroundings.

Word comes that the tuna are a couple hundred miles offshore. We head in to sell our salmon and switch our gear for tuna. In the Bay Haven that night, bursts of laughter break out as forty hands slap the tables.

But a north wind sidles down the coast and keeps us in port for a couple of weeks. I hang in the bars with many of the other fishermen who are also stuck in port.

I meet Bruce. Eddie calls him the Adonis. Dark hair and eyes, built like Schwarzenegger. He appeared in Newport with the eastern onslaught of fishermen when scallops were discovered off the coast. We meet playing 4, 5, 6 at the Abbey Lounge, throwing dice across a felted board as another player yells, "Baby needs new shoes." Bruce and I find an immediate commonality in our funny accents, his Boston and my Long Island mixed with Oregon. We hang around together, drink together. But he has a girlfriend back East, and she has a kid. We vow never to sleep together.

And then I wake up next to him, the only covering I have is on my tongue. I know Bruce loves me and he'll leave her. He said so.

CHAPTER EIGHT

Eastern Pacific Ocean

Back at sea, I find a rhythm of sorts and again, time begins to fold in on itself. Day nine is the same as day three was, and isn't any different than day fourteen or thirty-six will be. There's only sunrise to sunset. Only Phil and me with a few fish and the sea.

The tuna have disappeared, other than a straggler now and then. I'm as bored as I was salmon fishing. I spend hours on deck, between bites, asking the ocean what it is it needs to tell me. What message does it have to relate, and in what language? I want to understand why I'm here, on this boat on this ocean. At times, when I give up asking and listen, it seems near. But when I grab for it, it's gone.

One benefit of coming out is that I get a break from drinking. Phil's asked me if I want a beer, but that would be drinking for the flavor, and who drinks for the taste?

I never know where we're going next. Phil doesn't, either. We follow the fish reports from the radio, or look for the warmer currents the tuna ply. A line of color stretches for miles where the water warms, one side gray, the other green. Similar but opposing forces, repelling each other's touch, yet dependent on one another for existence. It's two people, constantly pushing against each other, yet clinging — a samba.

We're fishing with the fleet again. The radio is alive with the chatter I once thought I never wanted to hear again. They're making plans that change daily, sometimes hourly. The captains make up their minds as a group to go to Vancouver Island. No, maybe Monterey. Plans and counter plans. Where will the fish turn up next? Where's the next bite? Maybe we'll stay here for a day or so. Maybe the change of the moon will get the fish biting again. With a light pencil, I plot courses on charts to this place and that. I erase and re-plot. But the fish aren't biting. Ten days out on this trip and already I miss human touch. Other than once a day when Phil nudges my shoulder to wake me from my nap, there is no contact. I sleep in his bunk during the day because it's too loud in the foc's'le.

I miss life. Here, I have no problems, no people, no deep conversations over a glass of wine. Just cold, wet and tired.

There is no sun –– the clouds swept across the blueboard of the sky five days ago and erased it, leaving an ethereal chalk. Each night, the light is swallowed by the western horizon, and the day gives way to complete darkness.

I think about quitting, but I can't do that. It would mean defeat. The summer will have been wasted. I wonder what the hell got into me, taking this job in the first place. Crazy. Still, I have a sense that this is the way to Dad's heart. Even though I'm hundreds of miles away, I feel close to him in a way I never have. I think back on the fishing conversations we had that each seemed longer than all the conversations of my life, combined. I'm lifted by the thought of sharing stories when I get home.

We get to shore and sell our meager catch. Even though my bank account isn't much bigger, I feel good. The ambiguity of the lonely days at sea is gone. There's a sense of accomplishment, I'm a fisherman, fair and square. I take the bad with the good and can brag about the good catches and commiserate about the ones that got away. I'm a part of the fleet. I forget how miserable I was, and am ready to do it again.

CHAPTER NINE

Eastern Pacific Ocean

Growing up, there wasn't any real conversation in my house. Children were to be seen and not heard. Most communication was between kids, bickering about who used the last of the hot water or who stayed on the phone too long. Parental discussions were to be avoided because they typically meant there was some chore to do, or we were in trouble. I guess maybe that's why I have no talent for chitchat. If you asked, I'd say small talk is a total waste of time. Inside, I crave the ability to converse, even though it makes me excruciatingly uncomfortable. I think of what to say that might sound smart at the same time someone else is talking. I want to be witty, but end up off-key because I didn't get what the other person was saying while I was thinking about me.

My family and I exist in the same place and time, but where our spirits and minds are concerned, we live in parallel universes. Even though I love my family at a bone-deep level there's never much to say to one another.

My mom has a lot of faith in my ability to be independent; as long as she thinks I'm with my brothers, I'm given free will. I use this privilege frequently.

Then there's my father. He intimidates me. He can laugh and joke with the best, but he can't show that he loves me. When I was little he showed affection, but something changed when I began tripping over my feet and my face freckles broke into pimples. No more rides on his foot. The already minimal physical contact we'd had stopped completely. No more, "See ya later Alligator."

The solitude of the ocean is appealing to me. There's this intimacy at the same time there's no expectation of getting to know details about the person I live with. Here on the Valhalla, Phil and I have this comfortable silence. I feel like if I have something to say I can say it, but I don't feel like I have to attempt banal conversation.

A couple of weeks into the fishing trip, I'm filthy and Phil allows that I can use fresh water to bathe. I'm certain this is a bow to my femininity, but I gladly take advantage. Salt air, perspiration and fish blood are dried in my hair. My pants and the light denim jacket I wear — the one that once shouted style — are covered in fish blood. They're full of viscera and stiff to the touch. Having no laundry or shower on board means day after day in the same smelly coating. I feel like I'm dressed in a poorly tanned muskrat skin, like I've bathed in a swamp. Although I'm too close to myself to smell me, I know I'm foul.

In the morning, I leave two pots of fresh water on the engine manifold to heat. When the day's done, I carry the precious liquid up the ladder, one container at a time. Phil goes to the wheelhouse, promising to stare straight ahead while I go to the back deck. I peel my clothes off and add hot water to cold in one of those garden watering cans — the green plastic ones with a flower embossed on the side. I pour warm water over my flesh.

It doesn't wash over me as much as it dribbles. The slime of the past weeks slides down my skin to the deck, along with crust and scales. I lather up and rinse in minutes. I'd love to luxuriate in the scent of Ivory but the night air is chilly and bites at my skin. I dry off, and put clean sweats on. Clean is relative here, meaning only that I haven't fished in them. I return to the cabin and wash my hair in the sink, a new woman.

We work through the summer months. Sometimes we catch, sometimes we don't. We go to port and offload fish, load fuel and groceries and head back out. Newport, Eureka, Moss Landing. Now of legal age to drink, I take advantage of the nightlife in port.

There's a blow and we're stuck in Eureka for weeks on end. At the Vista del Mar I practice my pool arm and my drinking elbow. Affectionately known as the VD, it's the only bar in town, as far as the fleet is concerned. It's dark and dreary so it holds a sense of anonymity, but nobody much cares how sloppy you get, and in the small community of fishermen, there's no invisibility. I take full advantage of my sense of freedom, and I stumble home to the boat every night, alone. I don't want Phil to get the idea that I'm loose or anything. For some reason, his opinion of me matters deeply.

By June, the blows have settled down, and we're back to fishing. We do okay for the next month, and we head north, off of Newport.

In the late days of August, a mist appears over the water in the mornings and evenings. Sometimes it's fog, thick and heavy like a veil of white tulle piled softly over the sea. At times it's an ethereal ghost, undecided about whether to take form. On this particular evening the smoky vapors curl and snuggle up against the surface of the water in wads of white cotton candy, hugging the low swell. Other than these pockets of fluff, our visibility is excellent. It's a perfect summer evening.

We're sitting down at the galley table, Phil and me, having dinner. Phil sits facing starboard and I'm next to the door, facing forward. His hat's off to eat. Tonight he's cooked a pork roast with broiled potatoes and frozen mixed vegetables — the kind with green beans tossed in alongside limas and peas and those perfectly cubed carrots. As we do every night, we have sliced Franz bread with margarine, alongside a salad of iceberg lettuce and tomato, with a choice of Kraft Thousand Island or Russian dressing. Phil likes pork and cooks it often. At first, I wouldn't eat it – the smell of it sent me to the edge of the boat, my insides wailing. Tonight, I manage to nibble at the rim of the meat, but mostly eat the vegetables and potatoes. I have to eat something. I've lost fifteen pounds, and my pants are starting to fall off. You'd think I'd mention something to Phil. If I would, he'd likely cook something else. But in cowardice masked as politeness I say nothing, other than "it's seasickness."

We're at trolling speed, close to eight knots, or around nine miles per hour. Every few minutes one of us gets up to check the ocean around us. My turn. I go up to the wheelhouse. I look for other boats or anything drifting in the water that might do the ship harm. Could be something clearly visible like painted wood.

It could be something almost invisible like a deadhead — a waterlogged tree that's partially submerged, leaving a bludgeon on the surface. I walk back and check the deck for the same, and peek out to see if we have a taut line from a fish bite. All seems well, and I return to the table.

"How many fish do we have in the port bin?" he asks as I sit down.

I consider the question while I take a bite of vegetables.

"Well, I started using it yesterday, and put about two hundred fish in. I added eighty today, so a total of... two-eighty. The brine seems to be holding up. I think we'll be okay."

Right. Here I am, barely a novice at this work, and already an expert. I'm embarrassed at my presumption.

But he doesn't notice. He acts like I've been doing this all my life. "Well, that sounds about right," he says. "Let's leave them be for tonight. We'll start using a starboard bin tomorrow."

I'm relieved. It's totally creepy to go down in the hold and rearrange dead tuna. Bug Eyes, we call them. They stare vacantly, yet accusingly. Hundreds and hundreds of fish I've killed, all in one small, dark place. Them and me.

Plus, I'm tired. I want to eat, get the evening bite done, throw any new fish in the hold and wrap things up. I have at least two hours of work left, and rearranging fish would add at least another hour to that.

We have a few moments of comfortable peace, like two old friends enjoying the quiet at the end of the day. I feel like I belong, as if I'm part of the conversation. A part of the decisions, like my opinion matters. I like it. A lot.

The ship lurches. My ribs are forced into the table and my head jerks forward. I suck in a painful breath. There's the sound of wood splintering.

"We're hit," Phil yells, and I see fear in his eyes.

We both jump up from the table. My instincts take me to the deck. Phil's experience drives him to the wheelhouse.

The bow of another boat, a trawler about fifty feet long, leans into our broken port rigging. Her lines are caught up in our trolling poles and lines; she can't straighten herself. We're in a cloudless, fogless evening surrounded by the soft glow of a barely setting sun. Conditions couldn't be better. But here we are in a crash 200 miles from home and I don't know if we're sinking. I see a deckhand on the other boat. He's on the bow, doing something with the lines.

I'm cold and my ribs hurt with every breath I take, but I need to do something. Every piece of me is ready to spring, but I have nothing to spring toward except water.

I look for Phil and see that he's left the wheelhouse for the forward deck. My ping-pong brain takes over, bouncing from the boat and what to do and where to be. Fear and urgency collide.

"Are we sinking?" I yell to Phil.

I'm sure he hears me but he doesn't answer. My God. We must be sinking.

Phil runs aft along the port side with a knife and I back away. He reaches over the side and cuts through our trolling lines, almost freeing the other boat. I see the other deckhand working lines, hopefully untangling them.

"Are we sinking?" I ask Phil again.

He says something but I can't hear it.

The wood is making a low-pitched squeaking sound like a moose in labor. The boats are pushing against each other with their individual tons of weight. Our pole is snapped and looks like a grasshopper's leg, dangling over the other boat. My brain continues to bounce from the boat and what to do and where to be, to the one and only survival suit, and how quickly I might get to it, and will it really be mine as Phil promised.

"Got that line cut over there?" Phil yells to the other deckhand.

"One to go."

One final moose-squeak and almost as quickly as we'd tilted, we right. The boats continue to rock, a little less with each undulation.

The Valhalla II ends up with a wound in her port side, midship, above the waterline. The other boat has damage to her starboard bow. We're out of danger of sinking, but our trips are over.

We head for home, and I expect Phil will light into me about what happened. How could I have been so stupid? How could I have missed that boat? Phil will fire me for sure. It's got to be thousands of dollars worth of damage.

But, Phil says nothing. He's not even mad. Technically, it was the other boat's fault because we were on her starboard side. Still, I feel responsible. I should have seen them. I should have taken more time, rather than wanting to eat and finish for the day. What am I going to tell people? The boys? Dad?

On my watch that night, the ocean is calm, but the boat glides clumsily upon her. It's like we're traveling over a series of rolling pins that are hidden beneath a crushed velvet blanket.

In an attempt to avoid thinking about the upcoming conversation with Dad, I take my hair out of its usual ponytail and spend time on the important work of separating split ends. I take each strand, one at a time, and bring the tip up to see whether it's begun to split. If it has, I take both edges and carefully pull them apart. While I'm searching for the next end to attack, I find a grey hair. I hold it between my thumb and forefinger, considering what I've heard: for every gray hair I rip out, seven will take its place.

I yank at it, feeling the bite to my scalp, and then drop the offending strand to the deck.

Phil takes the watch in the early evening. I head for my bunk below, and fall asleep immediately.

And the dream... it comes again that night. Someone or something is chasing me. I'm doing okay outrunning it, but when I get to the door of the house, I reach out, but can't touch the handle. I try to stretch my hand out further to gain that last inch, but the handgrip is always outside my grasp. The monster is gaining. I scream. But the only noise that comes out is a guttural "uhhahhw." I wake myself with that sound. I'm out of my bunk, reaching my arms through the overhead hatch into the night air, trying to shove my body through. The noise of the engine is on my side; Phil can't hear.

I almost finish the season. I'm supposed to stay until September, but I'm drawn home in August. I'm homesick. In Moss Landing, California, I tell Phil it's my dad... he needs me at home, but I don't say why.

I pack my sea-bag, leaving the matching set of sheets aboard, throwing away the destroyed clothing. The bus takes me to San Francisco where I spend the night in a walk-up hotel room with a shared bathroom down the hall. It's luxury from my point of view. The next day, I take another Greyhound, North to Portland and then Southwest to Newport where Dad will meet me at the station. South of Roseburg, I lose focus on the book I'm reading, and notice the uncomfortable seat. I have second and third thoughts about quitting. Dad's going to think I'm a quitter – that I can't keep a job. And it's true; I've never held a job for more than a year. Most of my high school friends are half-through college and here I am, quitting a fishing boat that hasn't gotten me any closer to being better or smarter than who I was.

In Newport, I stand outside the bus, watching as the driver removes luggage from the outside compartment. Dad walks up and stands four inches from me. He never did have a sense of personal space. For someone who won't touch me, he gets awfully damn close. My muscles tense like they do the second before I dive into cold water on a hot summer day.

"What happened, Sha?"

I'm afraid to tell him that I missed home. Afraid to say the words I can barely grasp in my heart, I need a connection with you, a physical strand that I can see and hear and touch.

"I was tired of getting seasick, Dad."

He's disappointed, I can tell by the way his jaw wiggles forward, then right to left. Or maybe he's readjusting his cigar. "That's too bad, Sha. Sometimes the small boats are tough," he says. "The bigger ones don't bounce around so much, and once someone gets used to the ocean, they don't usually get sick."

I don't talk about the collision.

CHAPTER TEN

Newport, Oregon

That night, my 1967 Pontiac coughs black smoke and dies. I borrow my mom's car and go out to the Bay Haven and then to the Pip Tide.

The night starts out well enough, a couple of beers and a game or two of pool at the Bay Haven, then on to tequila down the street. Bruce is with another woman, and I'd very much like to make him jealous, but can't get another guy to pay attention to me. I'm angry, I'm depressed. The alcohol has its way with me. My life is senseless, a true waste. I get into the car and drive. My final destination is the Pacific at the cliff near Jump Off Joe. It's a long drop to the ocean below. I need to get Bruce out of my head. More importantly, I need to get me out of my head.

Pathetic, this driving a car borrowed from my mother to kill myself.

I arrive at the intersection of Highways 101 and 20. It's a green light, I can drive right through.

There's a blue car, coming from the north. Without stopping, he makes a right on red.

How dare you! It's my right of way!

I step on the gas. Not a lot, but enough to ensure contact. Teach them a lesson.

Crash! A jolt as my skull meets the headrest. Metal hits metal. More contact than I'd anticipated. Rage pumps blood to my ears, deafening me.

The front grill of my mom's little red car sits a few feet closer to me and now sports a V-shaped hood. The blue car pulls into the Oregon Maid ice-cream parlor parking lot; I pull in behind. We each open our doors at the same time. I lunge, screaming, "I had the right of way, you goddamnmotherfuckingbastard! Where the fuck did you get your fuckingdriver'slicense? I can't believe you fuckingpulled out in front of me like that. Are you fuckingstupid?" Flailing hands, staggering stance, wild eyes.

53

Mouth slightly open, the other driver says nothing as he begins to assess the damage to his vehicle. His passenger stays in the car, eyeing the situation. I march back to my running car, leaving them in a dazed stupor. Rubber squeals.

I continue my trip to the ocean.

Six blocks down, a siren squeaks — one short, attention getting squawk. Blue lights flash in my rearview mirror. I pull to the side of the road, about five blocks short of my intended destination.

"Shit!"

An officer is at my window.

Aw fuck! It's Frank.

Frank, from Mo's. He came in to visit all the time. Shit!

I assume he's pulled me over because of the hit and run.

There's a shimmer of recognition in his eyes as he informs me that he's pulled me over because I have no headlights. Ignoring this information, I speak out from the place in my subconscious that has a desire to live.

"Take me in. Guilty."

"What did you do?"

"Hit and run. Guilty. Take me in."

"Calm down. Tell me what happened." Frank has a concerned look about him, and it's clear he'd rather be anywhere but here at this moment. He takes his police hat off and wipes his brow with the back of his right hand. The crescent of hair surrounding the shine on top of his head has always been endearing to me. Frank is a nice guy.

"Hit and run. They pulled out in front of me, so I hit 'em. I stopped and yelled, and then I left."

"Well, that's not hit and run. You stopped."

"Drunk driving then. Guilty. Take me in."

"Okay, Theresa, wait a minute." Defeated in his attempts to save me from myself, Frank walks back to his patrol car.

The sound of the crash echoes in my head along with the sound of my voice, screaming obscenities, interrupted by a siren.

I rip myself back to the present and realize I'm more afraid of the humiliation of being arrested than I was of killing myself.

Tears fall down my cheeks, along with a disgusting stream from my nose. I use the backs of my hands and forearms to roughly swipe at the mess. The goo smears my cheeks, hands and arms.

Frank returns.

"Theresa, I'm recording our conversation now. I'll need to see your license and registration."

I scramble through my wallet and the glove box, consider my strategy, and hand over the documents.

"Will you repeat what you just told me?"

"Excuse me, officer? What did I tell you?"

Frank's tone is accented with a disappointed, downward flowing inflection as he asks, "How much have you had to drink tonight?"

"Nothing! I wouldn't drink and drive."

Accusation strangles the air between us. I can't believe you could say such a thing. The scent of tequila radiates out from the car, and from my breath.

"Okay, Theresa, I'm going to take you home now. Is your dad there?"

Dad? Not Dad! No way he can see me like this.

"Thanks, but my friend lives down the street — you could take me there." I completely avoid the topic of my parents.

CHAPTER ELEVEN

Newport, Oregon

Proclaimed as the home of winos, dingbats, and riff raff on the sign above the outside entry, Newport's Barge Inn is mostly an old folks' tavern. People whose goal is to get drunk alone sit at the bar, strategically placing themselves enough stools apart to allow a smattering of off-hand comments and gossip, but not so close as to allow any degree of intimacy. It allows them to either get away from their nagging partners, or to proclaim they don't drink alone. I'm here because the line at the pool table at the Bay Haven was too long for me. The Barge is mostly empty at 2:00 in the afternoon. Other than a couple of guys playing pool, there are a few fat, beltless butts spilling over too-small barstools. The bartender faces a silent television screen, I get her attention.

"Hey Annie, got a dark beer?"

She doesn't answer, but walks toward the tap, not turning her head from the screen until the pilsner glass is in her hand.

I put my quarter on the pool table, beneath the bumper and above the coin slot, reserving my place in line. No other quarters up. The unspoken pool house rules say that I'll be next against whoever wins this game. I walk over and sit at the bar to wait my turn.

The beer arrives, a dark ochre color. The heft of it suits the wet and gloomy winter in Oregon, a season that takes up most of nine months.

This guy comes in the door, and he's walking toward me. It takes a minute to place him. I've seen him around and heard plenty about him; he's a captain. Buddy's boats are high-liners, meaning they're among the highest earning vessels that make as much or more than the rest of the Alaskan boats combined. Slots on his vessels are among the most sought after in the fleet. These guys can make a hundred grand in a few months.

He takes a stool, two seats down, and smiles at me. If I were less naïve, I'd recognize it as an oily smile. His hair is dark and parted to the side, controlled by Brylcreem. He smoothes it down, pushing it against his scalp, then makes sure his side part is straight, using a comb from his pocket. With his hand covering it, he makes a swipe down each side of his head, then smoothes it down one final time.

"Hey." from Buddy.

"Hey, how's it going?"

"Good. You?"

"Awright."

That's the style. Polite. Minimalist. Sorta size each other up for conversation. A way to engage without engaging, talk without saying anything. We make half turns with our bodies to pick up or set down our beer glasses every few minutes.

Buddy's in his forties or fifties. A stocky guy, he's developed a paunch from too many years in the wheelhouse. He's about 5'10". Back to back, he's taller than me, but he seems much higher. Buddy has the demeanor of someone accustomed to giving orders — and having them followed. He sits on the bar stool, impossibly relaxed. His elbows lean on the bar behind him, his knees splayed open, not a care in the world. I sit, one barstool between us, hands folded on my lap, knees together. I lean imperceptibly toward him to show an interest in whatever he might have to say.

Silence sits between us as the pool balls carom off each other, sometimes dropping into a pocket. Then the sound of the ball rolling along the slide to the far end of the table where it's imprisoned behind battered acrylic. Gumballs, waiting for two quarters to free them. The cigarette smoke from around the bar converges over the table; creating a small weather system of stratus clouds. Some of it carries a blue haze that covers the table like the mists in the Hound of the Baskervilles.

The eight-ball hits the corner pocket, teeters on the edge, and falls in before its time. Ouch. Smallish groans escape the players. I stand up to take my turn. I nod toward my opponent and give a slight smile. He smiles back.

Walking toward the table, I reach into the pocket of my Levis and pull out a quarter to add to the quarter I've already put on the table. I put both of them into the slot, side-by-side, heads up for luck, and push the metal tab into the slide mechanism. The ten or so balls that had been pocketed during the last game come rolling noisily out to the receptacle at the end of the table. I take the two steps to that end, bend down and grab the balls, two at a time, and place them on the green-felted top. My opponent sweeps the other balls with the butt end of his stick, moving them toward my end. I pick up the triangular wooden rack and place the balls inside, alternating solids and stripes, eight ball dead center.

All the while I'm sizing up my opponent. He's relaxed — he's thinking he can beat me, no problem. I've seen him play, and he's okay, but I'm sure I can win. His right arm — the one holding the butt of the stick — has a tendency to sway before he hits the ball, leaving him with little control. Add to that the problem of a relaxed left hand around the tip of the stick and his control decreases even more. I have an advantage in that he's never seen me play. I gently pull the rack up and away from the triangle of balls and slide it back into its slot.

I walk toward my rival and offer my hand for a shake.

"Theresa," I pronounce.

He takes my hand and gives it a return shake. Firm, but not strong.

"Hi. I'm George. Ready?"

"I think so."

He walks to the cue ball, picks it up, and places it on the table behind the worn out circular patch that marks the edge of the area he's allowed to shoot from. He takes the cube of chalk and squeaks it solidly against the tip of his cue. Blue powder falls, dissipating into air.

He hits the cue, and it rips into the rack. The balls fly to all corners of the table. The seven ball clackety-clacks into a side pocket, giving George the solids to shoot. He surveys the table, and then walks over, intent on the two. He hits it, but it misses the corner by an inch. My turn.

He's left me set up for the ten, but I don't see a shot after that. I could try for the ten with a set-up for the twelve, or deliberately miss the ten-ball, leaving him without a shot. I opt for the latter, and George takes a long time to assess the table. I return to my beer, giving him his space. Buddy is watching the game.

"Nice leave." he says.

"Thanks, he may have a shot at the three."

"Nah – he's not that good."

Buddy's right, George misses the shot. This time, he's left the table wide open for me, and, one by one, I hit the balls into the pockets, including the eight. Game. George and I shake hands again, and he goes back to his seat at the other side of the bar to nurse his pitcher of beer. Nobody has a quarter on the felt for the next game, so I sit down next to Buddy again. Queen of the table.

"Nice game – you creamed him. Don't have much mercy, do you?"

I smile.

"Heard you know how to cook."

"Well, I cooked down at Mo's, and for my family, but that's it."

"Heard you worked on the Valhalla."

"Yeah, but Phil did most of the cooking." I did cook some, but I don't think it matters – it was just the two of us. Besides, I was mostly a deckhand. I'm proud of that fact, and don't want anyone thinking I was just a cook.

"Ever think about working up in Dutch?"

He's referring to Dutch Harbor, Alaska. The gold rush town of commercial fishing.

"My brothers've worked up there — Bob's up there now," I answer, as if he's asked me an entirely different question.

He responds to my denseness with a clear question, "Do you want to work for me this season — out of Dutch?"

I'm a bit light-headed now, and all I can say is, "When?"

"Next week. We're on a joint venture with the Russians."

My heart's rhythm begins to beat faster. My brain starts with a whispered refrain: Adventure... adventure. Gone the idea of 'just a cook.'

I'm nervous to ask about pay. If I ask, maybe he'll think I don't trust him to be fair.

But people will ask me, and I'll need to tell them something. I don't want to seem like a doormat.

Dad will ask. The boys will ask. They'll expect me to know. But, everyone makes good money in Dutch, he has to pay me a decent wage. Maybe asking will start us out on the wrong foot. I don't want him to think it's about the money. But if I don't ask him, maybe he'll respect me less, it might make me seem like a sissy.

I find my courage. "What's the pay?"

"Ninety a day – I'll need you for three or four months."

Although I hear the number, I don't listen. It's information for the sake of information. My mind's made up before he even tells me. "Sure," I say, afraid to say anything more.

"Gimme your phone number," he says as he pushes a pencil and a rectangle of white paper over to me. The lined paper has been perfectly torn from a larger sheet, as if it's been folded and creased, over and over, before tearing.

I write my number and hand it back to him. Buddy folds it once, right down the middle and puts it in his breast pocket, He picks up his glass, puts it to his lips, and empties it without ever taking his eyes off me. He places it soundly on the bar and stands. "I'll get the details to you. See you next week."

And that's that. That's really that. I'm going to Alaska. Just like that!

Then I remember seasickness, but I convince myself that it's done. I've given my due to Mother Ocean. It's a bigger boat and I'm used to the motion now.

The excitement builds from the bottom of my belly on up in a wave of warmth in my chest, exiting through my lips with the slightest Mona Lisa smile. As I leave the Barge Inn and review what's happened, I realize that Buddy came in looking for me; it wasn't random. He came in, sat next to me, chatted in his clumsy way, asked about the job and left. I walk toward the car, and my smile gets bigger until I'm laughing at my luck.

It doesn't occur to me that the crew might appreciate a more intimate knowledge of a galley than baking cakes and making burgers for my family, slinging chowder at Mo's, or throwing together a salad and pot roast for two.

CHAPTER TWELVE

Newport, Oregon

I'm twenty-four and, other than debts created when I ventured out on my own last year, I don't have many external complications, only internal ones that tell me to flee whatever place I'm in. This idea that I ought to get out before someone finds me out. It's better to quit than be fired. I'm living with my folks, so all I need to do is clean my bathroom and pick up my clothes. Likely they'll appreciate an indication that my life is headed in a positive direction. The Aleutian Islands are a step up.

Working on the Valhalla had been the impetus for that time when Dad really talked to me. Shared moments with the two of us having a conversation more in-depth than what's for dinner can be counted on one hand. Almost every one of those talks was created by fishing, defined by water. And even though these moments touch me deeply, they also, by their unfamiliarity, make me uncomfortable. I want to rush away from them but, at the same time, I want to find their depths and plunge.

Plus, I know Buddy doesn't put up with drugs on his boat, and I could use a break from those, and from drinking. Just some time to clear my head. I know I don't have a problem... I just need some time away.

Dad and I have one of our sit-downs. Our talk is at the same kitchen table, in the same chairs, as the last time. The heavy wooden table connects us and divides us at once. His White Owl New Yorker is a stub, but it fills the air with sweet-acid cigar smoke. With his lips, he pushes it over to the side of his mouth, then removes it. Between his pointer and middle fingers is the end that's been spittled and gnawed into shredded ribbons of tobacco wrap.

"You'll want to start thinking about jobs on boats in the Merchant Marine. Steady pay, safe vessels, travel the world. The boat I was on was the Archer T. Gammon. I was an able seaman up out of Seattle, heading back and forth to Asia. Then they put me on that troop transport in the army. We landed in Korea back in the 50's..." A pause. I think about this new information. Maybe if I go into the Merchant Marine, I'll have made it. Why is it always something more than what I have?

"Been to the Aleutians, too. Dutch Harbor, but we just called it Dutch. Used to say there was a pretty girl behind every tree. No trees in Dutch," he gives a half laugh.

"There were bunkers from WW II all over the place. Some of them still had ammo in 'em. Maybe they still do. You'll want to look in the hillsides for rocks that don't belong."

Now, I'm soaking it in. The feeling of being with him sits softly in my heart, along with the possibility of a closer, more meaningful relationship. I bask in relevance, the feeling of not being enough pushed to the back of my head.

"There were Russian trawlers back East in the sixties and seventies," he says. "I think you saw one from the Cricket II. They can be a thousand feet or more, and the crews work for up to a year at a time without ever getting to port. They don't get paid much, either. Maybe you'll be able to trade them for vodka. They like blue jeans, American cigarettes, and whiskey."

Out loud, he remembers the friends he made. Even though he's never seen most of them again, he feels a strong connection with them. "Life gets in the way." Later, I'll wish I'd paid more attention to this conversation, rather than just glowing in the feeling of togetherness. But I'm amped up with excitement about my trip.

I pack, bringing only what fits into the duffel bag that my brother has loaned me. While packing, Bob comes in with a silver bar of ski wax and throws it on the bed. I look up at him in a question. It's always a battle with these guys. Who'll say something first. I always lose.

"What's that for?

"Pack it, and when you get to the ship, see if your survival suit zips smoothly. If it doesn't, rub this up and down it until it does. Better yet, just rub it. Most of those suits don't get checked. If the boat goes down, those seconds count in whether you make it out." A trickle of cold hits my belly. I know it's the most dangerous occupation in the country, but talking survival suits makes it real.

"Thanks. I'll use it."

"And the duffel is yours. Looks like you'll need it for awhile."

"Thanks, Bob." And I squish the prideful smile that's inching its way to my lips.

"And one more thing. Now that you're going up North, you need to remember the rule. If you're hurt, or something goes wrong, you only tell Mom and Dad if they need to know. Otherwise, don't worry them. "If you do need to tell them, you start with, 'Everything's okay,' and then say what's wrong."

It's what Mom always says when Dad's had a diabetic reaction or when somebody's been hurt. Times I know I need to worry.

CHAPTER THIRTEEN

Dutch Harbor, Alaska

J ust before I leave home, I hear about a ninety-two-foot fishing vessel that sank in fifty-foot seas in Alaska. Thankfully, the crew was rescued. Somehow, this information is almost exhilarating for me. It's like the excitement that runs through my belly and makes me have to pee. Maybe being close to the edge is a new drug. Instead of making drama of drinking, I'll create it with another way of putting my life in jeopardy. Whatever it is, I feel alive.

I consider my good fortune at having the chance to work in this place I've so often wondered about. The place to which my brothers and friends have disappeared for months at a time. The place my father talks about in reference to my brothers with such pride. I wonder if he's now talking about me with pride.

Dutch is known for its wild-west atmosphere. Fishermen work hard, and then play hard in a place where nobody knows your last name. Perhaps they feel the proximity of death. Maybe they're acting out on the knowledge that one misstep is likely the path to eternity. There's also the anonymity – like Montana in 1800. Thousands of people come and go in a town that has a regular population of about two thousand. There's little to call community.

On the plane, I put my small carry-on in the bin above my seat. I smile at the two men who I need to cross to get to my seat. It's a bulkhead, so they don't have to stand for me, but it would be nice if they did. Not certain whether I should have my back or my front to them as I cross, I kind of squiggle myself side to butt past them as they make wild, goofy smiles at me. When I get to my seat, I turn and sit, then turn to face them again, "Hello." They look at each other and the man next to me turns back and says "he-lo," smiling even wider. The one in the aisle seat leans his torso out beyond his partner and grins, nodding his head.

Great. Booble and Bobble. My tongue pauses on each consonant as I hold one finger out to my chest. "Theresa," I say.

"Uh, Vladimir," as he points his thumb to his chest. "Vasily," and he shifts his thumb toward his buddy, never taking his gaze from me, never letting his smile drop. "Very pleased to meet you," he offers with intent, every syllable its own word. He tilts his head as if to ask whether I understand. My smile is half of my answer, and I tell him his English is excellent – almost like a native. Why do I lie about these things? His English sucks.

I'm reconsidering my decision to not drink on the flight. I don't want to show up for my first day of work drunk, but how can I not drink with these goofballs next to me? Maybe just a beer? No. If I have one, it'll be two and then another, and before I know it, I'll be drunk. I made a promise to myself and I'm sticking to it.

Settled in, I watch the remainder of the passengers board. As I'd suspected, not one other woman.

The two guys in my aisle are friendly. The one next to me has a face an angel would envy, except maybe his red nose. He's big, and I'm glad for the drop-down armrest that keeps my space, mine. Their Levis are so stiff, they probably make a swishing noise when they move, and their western style shirts might be in style in outer Wyoming. They are a caricature of what one might think is the fashion in Alaska. Everyone else on the plane is wearing faded blue jeans or Carhartts with a sweatshirt, and most have a baseball cap.

Even though they speak no English, they are adept at ordering whiskey, which they do frequently through the two-hour trip. Their smiles and laughter get more pronounced with each pass of the flight attendant. I figure now isn't the time to practice the few words of Russian I remember from high school.

Each time a flight attendant passes, I refight my decision to not drink. A never-ending push-me pull-you of yeses and no's. I read the in-flight magazine, do the crossword puzzle, cheating only a little, and look out at the clouds, bringing them to life as slumbering lions and fairies.

When the fasten seatbelt sign lights up and the flight

attendants begin their landing check, I ensure my seatbelt is securely fastened. I dutifully return my seat back and tray table to their upright positions. I look out as we descend through the cover of cinereal clouds. Turbulence picks up and my nerves make me chatty. I turn to face my neighbor, but remember he speaks Russian.

It's too late now to have that drink, I turn to the window as we break through the clouds. The view calcifies me – I grip the armrests, consciously refraining from digging my nails into my neighbor's arm. He and his neighbor are chatting away in their mother tongue and laughing.

The landing strip is one hundred feet wide – only seven-feet wider than the plane's wingspan. That leaves three and a half feet of wiggle room per wing, less than my own arm span. Ballyhoo Mountain towers 1,600-feet up on one side of the runway, and the boundary of the other three edges of is hypothermic water.

Ahead of the plane is the mountain, and we're headed straight for it. I close my eyes, but can't bear to keep them shut. That mountain gets closer and closer, and my wingtip seems inches from the rock cliff. Coming into view beyond the mountain is a pile of metal that has the general shape of a twisted airplane, rusting into the ground. Again, I close my eyes. Seconds later, unable to stand the suspense, I open them. I set my top teeth in line with my bottom teeth and, lips closed, inhale about half a lung full of air through my nose. I uncross my legs, keeping my knees touching, and sit straight up in my chair in order to give myself the appearance of calm, but the ability to go to crash mode the second the announcement is made.

I feel the bump of a landing. The wheels jump back up, then hit the runway again. And again. The jet engine blasts as it reverses direction and mixes with the higher pitched sound of wing flaps resisting the onslaught of air. The deafening racket hits my ears and I'm sure it's the pilot's last failed attempt to avoid the mountainside.

But we miss it. My sober heart and stomach try to return to their natural position, but I can tell it'll be a while before I'm back to normal.

There's a blast of cold as the cabin door is opened to the outside air. Everyone gets up and quietly waits their turn to get out. When I get to the exit, I look out. With Ballyhoo behind us, I see nothing but gray and some snow covered hills to the side. It's like everyone told me, but it's different through my own eyes.

We disembark onto the tarmac in Alaska's January air, and then trudge quietly toward the terminal, mostly single file. I'd love to chatter with the guy in front of or behind me, but everyone acts as though they've been here a thousand times before, so I keep my gaze on the back of the guy ahead of me. But there are needles dancing along every nerve of my body, the tattooed message reading We're here! We're here! Let the adventure begin! I look around, taking snapshots of the scene in my head to report back to Dad. He'll love to hear about that rusted plane by the runway. I wonder if the terminal has changed since his day? That mountain sure hasn't. I also decide what not to tell him. Certainly not about my terror during the landing, or the loneliness of not having someone to share it with.

We walk into the airport, which is sparse and almost as cold as it was outside. I follow the guys, heading toward the right, and stand with them in front of a wide, steel bin adjacent to the wall of the building. There's a curtain of heavy-duty, clear plastic drapes - like the ones in front of the cooler case at the grocery store. But this one's designed to keep the chill out. It's ineffectual. It's January in the Aleutians, and cold.

The baggage begins to appear through the curtain and my fellow travelers start grabbing theirs. Along with the regular luggage, mostly in the form of army green sea-bags, there are lots of duct taped, cardboard boxes carrying items that are unavailable on the small island - engine parts and electronics, fishing gear. Vessel names are scrawled across the tops in black or red magic marker: *Alaskan Challenger*, *Bering Pride*, *Leslie Ann*. I've always been curious about the names of boats. Though the names of Buddy's boats are neutral, it seems that if fishing vessels don't have a woman's name, they have to have a rough sounding name, but nothing so tough as to enrage the spirits of the sea. We humans can be so superstitious and fishermen are no different. No whistling on board, lest one whistle up the wind. No plants on board, lest they seek the earth beneath them. No storing cans upside down, lest the boat try to right them. Most importantly, no leaving on a Friday. I've no idea why. The one adage I try to forget is that having a woman on board is bad luck.

My duffel bag flies through the curtain. I can tell it from the rest by a frayed hole next to the faded black lettering that spells USARMY. I've made a good choice, now isn't the time to stand out. Not any more than I already do. I walk up and grab it, sling it over my shoulder in the most masculine way I know, and head for the exit sign. After this trip, I promise myself a spree in Seattle for dresses and negligee. For now, I'll need to man up.

Coming through the door is a guy, walking with purpose. He's got short, curly brown hair and a thick, dark beard. He's dressed in Carhartts and a weathered-blue Alaskan Ship Supply sweatshirt. He zones in on me and walks over.

"I'm Hank. Let's get back to the boat."

Is that all? No 'Welcome'? No 'Glad you're here.'?

"Hi," I say before following him to a rusty white pickup truck. I throw my bag in the back, on top of some pipes and rags, and we drive for five minutes along a waterway that starts on our right. The cab exhales the smell of a crankcase and, could it be? Testosterone? I don't know, but it smells like my teenaged brother's clothes-littered floor.

Hank is good looking, but he doesn't seem to have much personality. He's shortish – maybe he has one of those short people complexes. But Dad always says, "When in Rome, do as the Romans do," so I keep to myself.

We cross the island so the water is now on our left. White caps sweep the gray surface. The truck's contents croak loudly on each pothole in the road. Conversation is, thankfully, difficult.

We pass a row of battered wooden buildings with a boardwalk out front, and Hank points his finger to the right, crossing over me as if personal space didn't exist. I follow with my eyes as he plays tour guide. "Unisea – bar, hotel, restaurant. Restaurant and bar are closed Sundays."

He drops his hand back to the steering wheel and moves his glance to the left, across from the bar, slightly lifting his chin,

"Grocery store. That's where you'll do most of your shopping."

A couple more buildings, and we're through. That's Dutch Harbor.

"Thanks. Do you get to town often?"

He says no and we travel in silence along the dirt road to Captains Bay, where the Mariner is docked. The island is as bleak as my dad said. Not one tree in sight. Hillocks are covered with snow and spots of windblown brown. Speckled here and there are clumps of dead grass, looking like dead chia pets. I think I spy what might be rock effacements camouflaged in the sides of one or two hills, but I can't be sure. I don't want to seem like a debutante, so I keep my mouth shut.

After almost ten minutes more, we come to a yellowish warehouse. Next to that is the dock, filled with boats tied not only to the dock itself, but rafted up alongside one another. There's a system of bad weather in the area, so lots of the guys are in. We park and head down the dock and climb over the Sally B to get to the Mariner. She's 98 feet long. I like the color, red – easy to see. She's steel and on her stern is a large cylindrical drum reel with orange and green trawl net wrapped around it. The deck is a combination of steel grating and wood that we cross to get to the house.

Inside, the ladder to the wheelhouse is directly forward. The galley is to starboard, and between them, the head, big enough to hold a shower. Hank points past the galley to a door on the starboard side of the boat.

"That's yours." He turns and leaves me to wonder what just happened. Well... I hadn't expected to be welcomed with a pea under my mattress.

I stand and stare. Every horizontal surface in the galley is heaped with dirty plates, cups, and condiments. The table is littered with home recorded videos and girlie magazines. What the fuck just happened? Where the hell am I?

"Welcome aboard," I mutter as I take the few steps to my room to stow my gear.

CHAPTER FOURTEEN

Dutch Harbor, Alaska

Inside the room is a bunk bed that runs the length of the opposite bulkhead, and takes up almost half of the quarters. The top bunk is stuffed with gear – it must be communal storage. The lower bunk looks like it's been recently vacated – sheets and blankets in a twist at the foot. A bright orange survival suit is out of its sack and on the deck. I set my bag next to it, leave, and close the door on the 70 square feet I'll call my own for the next three to four months.

I feel like a mail-order bride. I've come to a new country where I don't understand the language, customs or rules. I want to cry. I go to the sink and empty it to do the dishes.

After I've been at it for maybe an hour, there's a singsong "Hullo," from the door. I grab a towel and dry my hands as a nice looking guy comes in. He's dressed in clean Levis and his button-up shirt is tucked in. I smile a slice more than halfway. Welcoming, but not too welcoming. It doesn't seem like the place to be over-friendly.

"I'm Rick, are you the new cook?"

It's obvious, but he's cute, so I respond, "Yeah. I'm Theresa. Nice to meet you."

He looks at me for a couple of seconds and he has the kindest eyes. I like him.

"I'm the Russian interpreter on the Sulak. Is Buddy aboard?"

I want to tell him that I took Russian in high school, that I can say babushka and brat and strasfwetye. That the language is beautiful and I love it and I used to speak it until my tongue hurt. That my name is Tatiana Kienovna, Theresa, daughter of Kenneth.

"No, he's not due in until tomorrow. I'm the only one on board right now. Can I help you with something?" Hoping I can.

"No. I just came over to say 'hi,' and touch base. I'll be heading out tomorrow, so I'll catch him on the radio. How long have you been here?" He looks around at the still sloppy galley.

Embarrassed, I respond, "I got aboard about an hour ago."

"Ah. Looks like you've got quite the job on your hands. First time?" he looks at the corner of the television screen above the galley table, rather than at me.

"Yeah, Buddy hired me a few weeks ago. I'm looking forward to working here."

"I hope it goes well for you."

There's a pause and he turns to go, then turns back and his eyes pry gently into mine. "You take care," he says, holding my gaze until I break it in discomfort.

"Thanks. I will." And he's gone.

After more than two hours in the galley, I turn my attention to my quarters. I'd made a point of packing a few photos of family. I tape them to the bulkheads. Again, I've brought my own sheets, and I change them for the old. My clothes go into a drawer beneath the bunk, and my toothbrush, toothpaste and other toiletries nestle in on top of them so they won't bounce and roll around when we're under way.

I sit down on the deck and mindfully comb the survival suit for tears and holes. Called Gumby suits, they're made of a wet-suit type fabric — a little spongy to the touch. The average winter temperature of Bering Sea water is near freezing. If immersed, survival time might be seconds without a suit. A boat can sink in seconds, so knowing how to quickly get into a suit, even in the dark, is critical. I turn the strobe light on and off, then blow air lightly into the whistle, testing. I grab the ski wax from my gear, and rub it along the zipper. When I'm done, the zipper moves smoothly from bottom to top and back. Then, I put the suit on as fast as I can, pull the hood over my head, and zip up. I don't time it, but am satisfied with my ease at getting it on. I'll practice with the lights out later. Leaving it unzipped for rapid entry, I carefully fold the suit and stow it. I rearrange the crap on the upper bunk and stuff the suit in tightly so it won't fly out in rough weather, but not so tight that I can't easily haul it down if I need it.

Next morning, I'm up at five, making coffee. There isn't much to choose from for a meal, but I make scrambled eggs, bacon, and toast. The bacon is over done, but the rest of it's okay. My first meal - a success.

Breakfast comes and goes; I meet more of the crew. After Hank, who's the deck boss, there's Gary, who has hair the color of rye, parted on the side and straight as a sheet, about as thick, too. He has an angular face and is about my height. His eyes tell me nothing about him or me. He's the engineer.

Although I work on a per-diem basis, the rest of the crew works on a percentage. Both Hank and Gary get a slightly higher percentage because of their increased responsibilities.

John is a deckhand, and I can see why. Although he's just a few inches taller than me, he's twice as thick. He's enormous in the way of a rhinoceros. His body is completely muscle, but he has a certain softness that only big guys have, as if he lives to avoid offending. He has a sharp nose that softens toward the tip, and a heavy red beard. His hair's red and he's got blue eyes with reddish brown brows.

They all return my hello's, but none of them is particularly friendly. It puts me off balance – I don't know whether it's them or me. Are they unhappy with me, or are they jerks? All that's left is Joey who's Portuguese. He's supposed to arrive tonight.

I clean up from breakfast and inventory the galley, penciling a mark next to each item for the amount we have, and a blank space for the amount we need. Pickles, mustard, ketchup. Peanut butter, crackers. Eggs, butter, milk, flour, powdered milk. Anything and everything we could need for a few months at sea. No corner markets out there, no fast food joints.

The galley is the crossroads of the boat. Every trip to and from the crew's quarters requires a trip through. It's right off the deck, and the head and wooden ladder to the wheelhouse are right next to it. The cupboards are made of the same oak colored wood as the stairs and other trim. There's room for one person in the tight aisle that passes to the crew's quarters. When John or Gary comes through, they are quiet, but polite. Hank seems to force low-current electricity through the air when he comes through. He doesn't look any different, but it's like the decibels of his thoughts pierce the air and I want to be invisible.

Everyone is busy, getting ready for the trip. They're checking engine fluid levels, and making their own lists for spare parts. They check hatch covers and tie gear down.

After a few hours, Buddy comes on board and sits down at the mess table.

"How're things? Gettin' settled?"

"Yeah, pretty much. Learnin' my way around." I don't typically drop my g's, but here I am, trying to fit in.

"Let's see your shopping list."

I hand the inventory to him.

"I don't have a list – I mean, I know what we need, but I don't know how much."

"Let's go," he says as he rises from the table.

Buddy drives the same rutted road I'd come on with Hank, back to the grocery store. I'm not much of a talker to begin with, and now I'm certain that anything that comes out of my mouth will be the wrong thing. I wish Buddy would ask some questions, but he doesn't, so we ride in silence.

I'd gone shopping with Phil, but he just had me pick out some stuff that I liked, and it was just the two of us for a few weeks at a time. This will be six of us for three months. I know nothing about this, and even though I'd been honest with Buddy about my background, I'm lacking and am about ready to prove my ignorance.

Inside the Unisea, Buddy rolls a cart my way, then grabs one for himself. We walk down the aisles and he pulls stuff off the shelves and puts it into his basket, and points out items for me to grab and put into mine. The quantities are impressive. Although I've shopped for a family of six hungry kids at home, nothing prepares me for the volume. A case each of corn, beans, peas and mixed vegetables. Half a case of Bisquick and a case of peanut butter. A case of Milkman 2% powdered milk. Raisin Bran and Life and Cocoa Puffs.

We fill those carts and get two new ones. We move on to the pasta and get bags and bags of different noodles: Spaghetti, linguini, fettuccini, elbow macaroni. I don't know how I'll cook the stuff he's grabbing. Okra? I've brought *The Joy of Cooking*. I hope it's enough.

The frozen foods and dairy are last, and Buddy gives a guy in the office a verbal list. He'll box it up and have it delivered it to the boat tomorrow.

On the way out, Buddy stops at the magazine rack. He grabs almost everything in sight. He starts with *Playboy* and *Hustler*, each of which is covered with a woman in tanned skin and luxurious curves. I hope my face isn't turning red. He moves on to *Popular Mechanics* and other 'guy' magazines. After he's loaded up on that, he picks up a *Cosmopolitan*, which I think is sweet of him, but not really my style. What I learn is that, next to the porn, *Cosmo* is the most popular magazine here. Blatantly sexual with photos of beautiful women in minimal clothing, peppered with sordid stories about lingerie and foreplay, it's a celibate man's delight. Add to that the luscious scientific surveys rich in sexual content that read like a Harlequin Romance on estrogen and you have the equivalent of a Bering Sea Pulitzer.

Done shopping, we go next door to the liquor store. Buddy goes to the counter while I look at the offerings on the floor. Vodka, gin, scotch & malt, and my most recent personal favorite, Crown Royal. Buddy talks to the guy at the counter and I wish I could listen to how much he's getting, but I'm too far away to hear his softened voice. On our way over to the Unisea restaurant and bar he informs me that it's trading stock for the Russians.

"What do you get in return," I ask.

"Food. Or Russian vodka. Sometimes a sable hat. And sometimes we play poker and it's betting stock. The magazines are good trade, too. Of course, that's after we've gotten our kicks out of them." The warmth surges up my neck and into my face.

There's no one at the UniSea except the bartender. We sit at a table and order drinks and a couple of burgers.

I break the silence, "A guy named Rick stopped by yesterday. He said he's one of the translators."

"Whad'he say?"

"Nothing, really," but I remember his good looks and his gentleness. "He just said he'd catch you on the radio."

"Mmh."

"Is he our interpreter?"

"All depends on what boat we get." He looks around at the empty bar, and I mimic him. There are a couple of pool tables, but not much else.

The burgers arrive and we eat. I feel like I should talk, but I have nothing to say. Nothing that has anything to do with anything. Maybe talk about how it is in Dutch Harbor, but I don't know how it is. Questions about fishing seem silly, and again, the more I show my ignorance, the worse it'll be for me. I'll learn this stuff as it comes up.

A large woman with short, sandy-colored hair permed into tight ringlets comes in and looks around the bar, lights her eyes on Buddy and walks over to us. "Buddy, you old bastard! Why the hell didn't you tell me you were in town!"

"Just got in today. Susie, meet Theresa, my new cook." With a wave of his hand in her direction, he says, "Susie's our expediter. What we need, she can usually find for us. Have a seat, Suz." She and I smile at each other, but at the same time scope each other out. Competition? Can we work together? Is she a bitch? We look for all the information that's impossible to gather in ten seconds, yet we search anyway. I don't think much of her. She feels like a threat.

"Nice to meet you," we say in unison, but Susie roars, while my greeting's soft. I'm not accustomed to such expressiveness in people – it puts me off. She seems like one of those people who call other women 'honey' or 'doll.' She sits down and motions to the bartender, who fixes her a drink – it appears she's a regular.

She and Buddy start talking about the fishing season, and I listen. I take further stock of her, and begin to warm to her. She has an earthy way that I think I might like. She's relaxed and gregarious in a way I could never see myself. If I could dissect the moment, I'd say I have an attack of envy.

After about twenty minutes, Buddy stands up.

"Time to head back to the boat." He looks at me and I pick up my vodka with grapefruit juice to drain it.

"You have to leave so soon? We were just getting started."

Susie appears to be genuinely disappointed.

"Nah, I need to get some sleep tonight, get things settled before we leave."

"Why don't I show Theresa around? Have her back tonight, early? I'll keep her safe."

Buddy laughs. "Yeah – if she's okay with that. I'd love to be a fly on the wall for this one."

Unwilling to lose this opportunity to make a friend, I nod. "Sure, I'd love to."

Susie gives me a conspiratorial smile and shoos Buddy off with both hands.

Before Buddy's out of range, she turns to me as if he'd never been here.

"Let's finish up and head over to Unalaska and the Elbow Room – you haven't been to Dutch until you've been to the Elbow Room, even though it isn't in Dutch – HA!" Susie laughs at her own joke, and I give a little snort of uncertain approval. We get into her beat-up blue truck. She grabs a pile of paper from the passenger side and stuffs it behind the seat. The bed of the truck is full of boxes – she'd better hope it doesn't snow.

We take the rutted road a couple of miles over to the town of Unalaska, and the Elbow Room. Susie pulls up to the door and shifts the transmission to park, but keeps the engine running.

"You go on ahead in, Sweetie — I have a quick errand to run — give me about 15 minutes and I'll buy you a drink."

I hate being called 'Sweetie,' or anything resembling it, but at the moment, I'm more concerned about being dropped off at this infamous bar. If it were me, watching me go into this place alone, I'd assume I live in the shallow end of sanity.

I walk in and find it almost as empty as the Unisea had been. I stand near the entrance, adjusting to the dim light and the general atmosphere of the place. Frightened, I inhale and walk up to the bar with a confident step, take a seat, and order a beer. The bartender grabs a glass, pulls a draft for me, and sets it on the bar. I lay a twenty down, and he grabs it to make change. I take a sip and lick the foam from my lips as I look around the place. There's the famous bell that's rung when a patron who's feeling flush wants to buy the whole bar a round. Small, square tables are scattered about the place, empty. Black vinyl chairs with metal frames make it look like any dive bar, USA. But it's not just any dive.

Known all along the left coast as a 'must-visit,' the Elbow Room is like the Disneyland of the commercial fishing world. My brothers have all been here, and they've told me all about it. Well... maybe not all. But what they have said is plenty. The fights, the crowds, the all too masculine fun. The Elbow Room is rated as the second rowdiest bar on the planet, and the most dangerous in North America. Not that I know what the first rowdiest bar is, but Playboy does the ranking, and clearly that magazine holds a lot of sway around here.

The establishment's other claim to fame is that Jimmy Buffet played here once. I don't know whether it was a scheduled event, or he walked into the bar one night and started singing and playing, but guys still talk about that night as if they expect him to walk in again, any minute.

At this moment, none of the advertised danger is apparent, and I plan to be gone long before the fun starts tonight.

The bartender brings my change and sets it on the counter in front of me. I wonder what the protocol is. Do I tip him now, or wait until I'm done? Do I leave the cash on the bar for him to grab as he needs, or do I put it away it each time? For now, leaving it sit will be fine — the place is empty. But what if it gets busy and I need to pocket the money to keep from being robbed? If I pick it up after someone sits next to me, it'll look like I don't trust him. If I pick it up now, it might look like I don't trust the bartender.

I keep the money on the bar. I'd rather lose the change than look cheap or paranoid.

About ten minutes in, an old man with stringy black hair held in place by a rolled up, red bandanna walks up and stands at the bar, two stools down. He's dressed in a green vinyl jacket with faux fur trim. His feet are spread for balance, knees slightly bent under baggy blue jeans. The lines on his face are deep, especially those around his black-brown eyes. They are crevasses; sideways semi-circles, reaching down his ruddy brown cheeks. He stares at me. Not a threatening stare, more of a vacant gaze. He's plastered.

"Hi," I mumble when I'm sufficiently uncomfortable with his gaze.

He opens his mouth to reveal a two-toothed grin. Surprisingly, it's a beautiful smile that covers his entire face.

"Spell 'Tlinget'."

"Wh-what?" I ask.

"Spell 'Tlinget'." More demanding this time.

"T-L-I-N-G-E-T, Tlinget." Like I've entered some bizarre spelling bee.

I know Tlinget as an American Indian tribe, indigenous to Alaska. The t and l clink together and almost make a k sound.

The old Indian's smile returns, but bigger, seeming to reach halfway to his ears. His boozy-red eyes open wider. "You spelled it! You know how to spell it! Nobody even knows what it is, but you can spell it!" He laughs quietly, but deep into his belly, while shaking his head in disbelief as he walks away. I return to my beer.

In a few minutes he's back and sitting next to me at the bar, elbows outstretched like an albatross, head relaxing toward the wooden bar, looking forward. Terrific – a friend for life because I entered his spelling bee. But, always polite, I introduce myself.

He responds in kind. "Hi – I'm Jack the Tlinget – can't believe you spelled that. Gave you a prize. It's in the ladies room. First stall."

"What is it?"

"You'll see. Go on."

I consider picking my change up, but even a derelict deserves the benefit of the doubt. I get up and walk to the restroom.

Inside, the bathroom is bleak. Not dirty, but not clean, either. In the latex-coated stall, there's a small, rectangular white package on the toilet tank top, a razor blade alongside. I recognize the paper and its shape immediately. I open it and there's a pile of white powder in it. This guy has never met me and he's giving me coke. Where the hell am I?

But, who am I to question? I sit on the toilet seat, butt facing the door, and use the blade to portion out a generous mound. I straighten my leg to grab a bill from my pocket, roll it up and snort a long, deep sniff into each nostril. I stand and back away from the latrine, waiting for the rush to choo choo into my brain.

Seconds later, every care in the world has left me – even worries I don't know I have. They vanish. In their place is a feeling of inner peace I've never found without chemicals. A tingle spreads through my body. I take a breath of relief, knowing that I will be high for the next twenty minutes or so. Sweet.

I refold the rectangle and take it with me, back to the bar. I hand it under the counter toward Jack with a grin.

"Thanks!"

"It's yours, keep it."

"Jack — that's a gram of coke."

"No, it's more, and there's plenty more where that came from." Every 's' becomes a subtle whistle as it passes his lips beyond his mostly empty gums.

"Wow... thanks." What else is there to say?

The bar begins to fill and I'm the main attraction. John, then Guy, Bruce and Fred. A bunch of other guys vying for my attention; all of them want to buy me a drink. Although I'd accepted Jack's drugs, I knew he expected nothing in return. These other guys, however, do, and I want no part of it. I refuse all offers.

The level of noise and testosterone in the bar is rising exponentially with each 'set' that walks through the door. After a few hours it's clear that Susie got held up. I have the bartender call a cab for me, and I grudgingly leave the coke on the bar, figuring someone will either use it or throw it away. I want nothing to do with it on the boat. Although drunk myself from waiting too long, I have a smidgeon of sense left in me. Even though it might be everywhere in port, the Bering Sea is no place for drugs. Sure, some people use coke to stay awake for the grueling hours, but I know Buddy won't put up with that. I head back to the dock.

In the morning, I'm hung-over when the groceries arrive.

We've moved to a loading dock and the crew uses a net attached to a crane to swing the boxes of food from the docks to the deck. The stores are stacked on the back deck, then carried inside. I have to find a place for everything — spots where the worst rolling and knocking about won't dislodge them. The sound of a can of green beans, rolling from one end of a compartment to the other and banging against each bulkhead is worse than fingernails on a chalkboard. Not an experience I want to repeat after losing a can of deodorant in the foc'sle of the Valhalla.

I'm grateful that Buddy has done the majority of the shopping, even if I don't know what some of the stuff is, or how to use it. Still, I'm overwhelmed. Boxes are everywhere, and I can barely see over the top of the stack on the counter. Under the benches on the mess deck are storage bins, and there are cabinets above. But I don't know how I'll fit it all. I store cases of canned goods in my stateroom. There's milk: evaporated, powdered and condensed. The frozen foods have to fit in the freezers – one standing, and the small freezer on top of the refrigerator. There's freezer space in the hold, but if I want something from there, Buddy's told me I have to ask one of the guys.

On the back deck is a storage area called a lazarette, used for refrigerated items. This space stays cool but won't freeze. It's perfect as an additional refrigerator.

There's a cubby behind the angled ladder to the wheelhouse where I put potatoes, onions, bananas and cabbage. The only way I've ever used cabbage is at Mo's. We'd drizzle ranch dressing on top and add a few bay shrimp. I tasted it once and it grossed me out. What am I going to do with a case of it?

I meet Joey, whose English isn't so hot, but his eyes are a sparkling brown. Finally, someone on board who seems like he might be pleasant. He's Danny DiVito with hair and muscles. He's got a full black beard and wavy hair that swings when he moves his head. "Hi," he says. Although I can't see his mouth, I know he's smiling because his mustache stretches.

Next morning, I wake up refreshed and ready to go. The excitement is back; I'm heading into a new world. I'm sure the guys will warm up to me once we're out to sea. While I cook a breakfast of pancakes and sausage, they cast off the lines.

CHAPTER FIFTEEN

Bering Sea

Leaving Dutch Harbor, all boats go by Priest Rock. The bedrock sentinel blesses each outgoing boat as she passes.

If you mention this promontory to those who have passed it, I'm certain almost each one would get at least a tingle in their belly. Some would have a fire with embers that die down slowly, but never extinguish. Those who have passed by without incident may have a twinge of excitement that brings to mind the possibility of danger. Others — those who live with the fire — have returned from the Bering Sea, changed. Perhaps they've come back without a shipmate. It could be that they've been part of a search and rescue, maybe just the search. Priest Rock is only a rock, but it stands as a symbol. For Bering Sea fishermen, Priest Rock is legend. Not for any daring deeds done there, or mythic struggles; Priest Rock stands as the guardian between this world, and that.

We make it out of port, and take a left, staying in the relative calm of Iliuliuk Bay. We continue north through Unalaska Bay, where there remains a small measure of shelter, then we continue on into the open waters of the Bering Sea.

The first few days out are calm. Even so, I'm sicker than a Sunday hangover. I've got my Scopolamine patch behind my ear. I maintain hope for it even though it's yet to work for me. Heaving into the toilet or over the side, I'm a picture of abject misery.

Seasickness is like nothing else. It's not only my stomach — it takes over my mind and I become a different person. I don't care about anything, and want to find a hole to crawl into and die. It begins with a headache – not a super painful one, but it is persistent. Then comes the fatigue when I am almost powerless to stay awake. There's a fuzzy-headedness and things take a while to make sense. Things like how to turn a burner on, what goes first in the salad, how much ground coffee makes a pot. But, I stagger in to throw a casserole in the oven, or do a few dishes, then back to my bunk before the heaves start again.

To compound matters, the reality is more evident that my cooking skills are severely limited. I'm a novice. I told Buddy that I didn't know a lot about cooking, but he hired me, so I figured it was enough. These guys want stuff like okra, and they put peanut butter on their pancakes. The freezer is full of beef cuts I've never heard of, like brisket and foreshank.

In between meals like spaghetti, mac & cheese, and meatloaf, I cruise through *Joy of Cooking*, happy that I'd thought to bring it with me. I don't even know how to make coleslaw. I read through directions for beef stroganoff, and it's a success, I think. I stay in the galley while they eat because there's not enough room at the table. I watch them eat, looking for a sign of what they think of the food.

They have brief conversations. The engine is running, and it's tough to hear over it.

"How's that net repair holding?"

"Good," from Hank. "It loosened a bit on its first tow, but it's held since then."

Just the engine sound until a few minutes later when Buddy turns to Gary. "And that manifold? Did you get the leak fixed?"

"I'm still watching it, but nothing during the past few checks."

And then Buddy clicks a movie on, blasting its volume. I still don't understand the words over the engine, but the guys are glued to the screen.

Baking comes easier than cooking; I've been doing that since I was eleven. But not bread, and Buddy says that the other cook bakes bread. I feel obligated to make a loaf.

In *Joy*, there's an entire section titled About Yeast Bread Making. On page 553, cookbook authors Irma and Marion explain to me that yeast has a volatile temper and hates a draft. Yeast, they say, is decidedly feminine. They tell me I am the director of a staged play that stars yeast. They redirect me to the section About Yeast, page 503, where they discuss the fact that yeasts are living organisms, containing 3,200 billion cells per pound. I use a quarter of an ounce, pre-measured to perfection by Fleischmann. I read about how Spanish speaking peoples call yeast almas, meaning souls, because they're so spirited.

Enough education, it's time to get to the recipe. Straightforward is better for beginners, and page 556 has a recipe for White Bread Plus. Nine simple ingredients. In goes the yeast, along with a tablespoon of sugar, into warm — not hot — water. There it dissolves and bubbles to the surface; a minefield of exploding almas.

I add to this an egg, half a cup of melted butter, more water and more sugar. Oh... and salt. Mix. Pour into a well of eight cups of flour and place it all on the lightly floured countertop. We both get a rest for ten minutes. I spend my break time back on page 553 with a primer on kneading, the part I'd skipped reading.

As per the instructions, I fold the dough over, toward me. I then press it with the heels of my hands, as shown in the drawing. Give it a slight turn, fold and press again. Repeat 'rhythmically' until the dough becomes smooth, elastic, and satiny. This is where Rombauer, Becker, and I have a problem.

My hair and cookbook are covered with flour, my hands and the counter with paste. My dough doesn't look like the illustrations. It's not 'elastic' or any of the other adjectives they use. It's a blob that shows no difference from the lump of hope I've pushed and prodded, turned and coaxed until my arms are sore. Still, I retain my optimism and oil a bowl lightly and put the dough in, then cover it with saran wrap, and put it on the counter with a damp paper towel under it so it won't slide with a wave.

I look at it in an hour, and nothing is different. I move it closer to the oven and look in another hour. The same. After almost three hours, I 'punch it down' and put it in two aluminum bread pans to 'rise' one more time before placing it into the hot oven. Fifty minutes later, it's out of the oven, a beautiful golden brown, and as dense as a pile of wet cardboard. Over the side with it.

And so it goes. Failure after failure. Meat overdone, mushy pasta, burned sauce.

Even though I've fished commercially prior to this, and I've grown up with four brothers, three of whom have been commercial fishermen, nothing has prepared me for the months to come. The isolation, uncertainty and lack of voice over my destiny that now define my life are painfully clear. The next months, stuck on this boat with silent shipmates, loom in front of me. The noise of the engine hampers most communication, but a smile or a nod of acknowledgement would go a long way toward putting me at ease. I remember that it isn't anyone's job to make me feel at home, but it's little comfort. I feel like the last kid chosen for the team. The separation is magnified by the differences we experience in our work. Their work is physically demanding. They go out on deck and get the trawl net into the water while I stay inside cooking, baking, or cleaning.

My almas are low.

And although I don't mind leaving drugs behind, I don't like being without alcohol. But, I made a decision not to bring it with me. Lately, I've found it difficult to stop drinking once I've started, and I do not want to find that I've been out of control in the middle of the ocean with four men, aboard a boat. One of the few women working in the west coast fisheries, I believe I need to set standards to show that we women can work right alongside men, and not have "problems."

CHAPTER SIXTEEN

Bering Sea

The way trawl fishing works is this: The net is rolled up onto an eight-foot diameter steel drum, called a net reel. This is supported on the back deck by stanchions. When it's set out, the drum releases the cod-end first, a long sock-like net that has a mesh size of about an inch. This is where the fish go, after they've been funneled in from the larger net, called a trawl. The cod end is sewn to the trawl net with a strand of polypropylene line sewn in like a zipper. The top of the trawl is the head-rope, buoyed at a specific depth with foam floats. At the bottom of the net is the footrope, held closer to the bottom of the ocean by heavy rounds that look like donuts. They're made into disks from recycled tire rubber. On each side are massive steel panels, called doors. Altogether, they make the mouth of the net that funnels the fish into the thirty-five-ton cod end. An eel with a giant maw, eating everything in its path.

Everything on board revolves around the fishing schedule, which isn't a schedule at all. The guys set the reel and let the net soak until Buddy, using sonar and the feel of the boat under its load, decides it's full. Buddy rings the metal fire alarm and the guys head out to the deck. The crew uses a winch to reel the net onto the drum, then they draw the top of the fish-filled cod-end closed. They hook the cod-end to a line and the Russians transfer it to their ship and return it, empty. On a good day, they can fill a net in an hour. A transfer takes about an hour. At 35 tons of fish every two hours, that can be 400 tons of fish a day.

During net transfers, people stand on the deck of the Russian ship, looking down to see the Americans. We stand on deck, looking up to see the Russians. They're identical to one another from this distance, each in dark gray clothing that doesn't look like it can possibly give relief from January in these higher latitudes. And, even though their boat is almost ten times the size of ours, I find myself grateful for the relative freedom I have aboard our tiny vessel. Russia is in the throes of communism and all I hear about their country is that there is zero liberty, and abject poverty.

The weather on the Bering Sea is some of the most notorious in the world. Hurricane force winds pick up, seemingly without warning. When we hit a storm for the first time, I'm shocked by its violence. Sure, I've seen weather before. I've been knocked around and bruised from shin to shoulder. This is different.

The boat feels like a pinball machine; I am the metal ball being slung around inside. We go over thirty-foot waves, crest, and slide down the other side. That part is somewhat predictable; it's the waves that hit us on the beam that get me. They come without warning and slam into the side of the boat. I rarely have time to grab onto something, so am shot across the galley, stopping when I hit whatever happens to be on the other side. Times like this, I'm grateful for a small work area. But people have to eat. When it gets rough enough to slosh liquid over the top of a pot, it's too dangerous to work with hot food. At those times, we have sandwiches and cold cereal.

Nevertheless, I have to open the refrigerator. Try as I might, I can find no way to open the cooler door, grab what I need, and close it before something is thrown across the galley. I try to manage the task by working with the roll of the boat. Sometimes it works. It's like a tango with a malicious partner, keeping the perfect amount of tension between the wave and me at all times, while following my partner's lead. Once in awhile, my partner collapses just when I'm depending on him for support.

We're getting slammed. It's lunch time and I'm putting sandwiches out. The refrigerator door faces the bow, so I stand in front of it, legs spread for balance. Unlocking the clasp that holds it shut, I put my hand up against the door to keep it closed. As the boat hits the base of the wave, I move my hand to the handle. At the moment we begin the trip up the other side, I open the door and look frantically for what I need. I've made a mental list of mustard, mayonnaise, cold cuts, lettuce, pickles, and tomatoes. The meat and vegetables are easy, and I grab them before beginning the trip back down the next wave, when I close the door to wait until we hit bottom again.

The mustard is wedged next to the plastic pitcher of reconstituted milk; I retrieve it on the third roll. I allow the wave to slam the door shut, and wait for the next plunge to get the pickles. Things are jammed into the refrigerator in a delicate balance, keeping everything from sliding around, but momentum has its way. While the door is closed, the mustard hole allowed the milk to shift and swoosh over the lip of the pitcher, even though it's less than half full. I grab the container and put it in the sink; no way I can clean the mess up now.

I've got the door wide open when a beam wave hits and throws me off balance. Out fly a head of lettuce, two tomatoes, a jar of pickles and a plate of leftovers. The pickle jar breaks and the liquid acts like a tiny tidal wave, slopping toward the range, and under. The smell of acetic acid fills the galley. Everything skids and bounces across the galley deck, clashing and banging, rolling and sliding everywhere as I scramble to pick them up. One by one, I gather them and place them in the sink.

I learn the tastes of each of my shipmates. Hank likes his steak well done, John likes his almost raw. Buddy has eggs every morning, over easy, still runny. Ten days into the trip, he brings his breakfast plate down from the wheelhouse while I'm cleaning up.

"Give us some oil."

"What do you mean? You want a dish of oil?"

"Put some oil in them eggs when you cook 'em."

"Well, I do, but I'll put more in."

"Hmph." Grunt-like.

Next morning, I put maybe two tablespoons of oil in with his eggs, rather than one. Not a problem. I aim to please. It's not healthy, but it's not my body.

Down Buddy comes. "Honey, you need to give us some oil in them eggs!" 'Oil' is strangely garbled.

So, three tablespoons the following morning. I'm sure he can't possibly want more than that.

Down the ladder Buddy stomps, empty plate in hand. He's as

pink as the wing feathers on a flamingo when he turns to yell at me.

"Gawdammit! How the hell do ya expect anyone to take a shit around here? Use some fuckin' oil in them eggs!"

He doesn't lack for oil again.

Buddy is a drinker, but I never thought he'd drink at sea. Valhalla Phil would have a beer once in awhile, but that was different. I mean, beer isn't really drinking. Buddy – he drinks every day. Every afternoon, he has a glass of scotch. Then another, and another. It takes me awhile to tune into it, I've been so busy getting my sea legs and figuring out my place. But now it's plain as anything. I know when he's on his third or fourth because he starts to get friendly. He chats about people back home. Surprisingly, Buddy's quite the gossip — not that I'm unversed in talking trash about others. But my instincts tell me not to cross the invisible line into chumminess with this one.

Around week four, I head up through the wheelhouse to dump the trash. I've been instructed to use this deck so the person on the bridge can keep an eye on me in case I fall overboard. Not that there would be any help for me; if I went over, they'd have difficulty finding my dead body. I wouldn't last more than a few minutes in these waters without a Gumby suit on.

I throw the bag over the railing. After gagging on a few breaths of frigid air, I head back into the wheelhouse. Buddy stops me.

"Grab a glass – that cupboard over there." He points to an open cabinet in the aft of the wheelhouse, forward of the open door to his stateroom. I notice that his bunk is made like a Marine's. Tight, like a quarter could bounce on it.

I grab a glass and bring it over. He already has one, half full of amber liquid.

He reaches down to the open cubbyhole beneath the wheel and grabs the neck of a three-quarters empty bottle of scotch. With expert hands, he twists the cap off and pours my eight-ounce glass half-full with one graceful move, belying the amount he must have already drunk in order to ask me to join him.

I think about refusing, really I do. But that luxuriously velvet scent wafts up to my nose, reaches in, and seizes my olfactory glands. My insides dance with expectant ecstasy and my tongue oozes saliva.

Not wanting to appear too anxious, I sort of swirl the liquid around in the glass, watching the legs of the scotch cling to the sides like tentacles of sugar. I put it to my lips and take my first sip. The liquid hits the center of my tongue, collecting in a puddle. I release it ever so slightly, and it touches the inside of each cheek, then drops down in a waterfall, pooling on the outskirts of my gums. It travels to the back of my tongue, and takes the final plunge, into my throat and on down. I half close my eyes as I press my tongue to the roof of my mouth to squeeze out every. last. drop.

The burn begins. The burn that only whiskey gives – luscious and comforting at the same time that it is fire. Buddy watches, his brown eyes a hint brighter than they had been when I came in.

"Good, huh?"

"Mmhmm," I say dreamily, as I take another sip, my chest welcoming the warmth of my long absent friend.

Buddy is talking and I bring myself back in time to hear, "... things going? Getting along okay?"

"Oh, yeah - getting used to everyone and everything," I lie.

"You're quite the jewel, you know?"

"Well... thanks." Hesitant. I don't like where this is going. Not at all.

I take another drink, and am about halfway through the glass. Every inch of me is now a few degrees warmer, and I would be feeling blissfully relaxed, except for the building tension in the wheelhouse.

"You know, if it weren't for my wife, I'd chase you about anywhere." His body shifts toward me.

Small boat, getting smaller.

"Oops – dinner's gonna burn! Gotta go!" I drain the glass in one final draught and head down the ladder, empty glass in hand.

The rest of the day goes by in a happy blur. I think my

shipmates are the best, and though leery, I'm feeling philosophical about the captain, as well.

Sometime later, Joey comes into the galley. He's taken his orange Grundens jacket off, but has his suspender rain trousers on. In his hand dangles the head of a large fish. Skinny whiskers droop from its chin and its round, black eyes are ringed with a circle of amber. They lose their glassy appearance by the second.

"Can I use a pot?"

"For that?" I don't even point. I take a glance down at the head and then look back at those Portuguese eyes. "Do you want me to cook it?" Oh please say no.

"No. Family recipe. I'll cook it."

"Sure, but I'd be happy to learn." I talk fast, hoping he doesn't respond in the positive. "Let me clear this stuff and take a break so you can have the galley."

"Thanks." There's that mustache, rising again.

In my room, I wonder why he wanted to cook it himself. Not that I wanted to boil his fish head. But am I that bad of a cook that he doesn't even trust me to boil a fish head?

At dinner, it's clear that Joey is the sole revolter from the standard galley fare.

CHAPTER SEVENTEEN

Bering Sea

After forty-nine days at sea, we come into Dutch Harbor for a three-day turnaround. I'm on my own grocery shopping. I show Buddy my list and he makes a couple of changes - adds condensed milk and butter, reminds me about the magazines.

I pass the liquor store on my way to the grocery store. All the time I'm shopping, I think about how nice it was to have that drink. On my way back, I pick up two bottles of Crown Royal and spirit them away with the groceries. No one needs to know. Liquid almas.

Back at sea, I'm keeping to my promise of one, maybe two, drinks a day. This is going to work. It relieves stress, and at this rate, two bottles will last the trip.

My other stress-relieving activity turns out to be kneading, and I bake bread a few times a week. Push, turn, fold. I learn to make the dough elastic. I don't know what the secret to it is, but my wrists and hands learn. The galley is the perfect spot for the baby yeasties to rise, and I love the smell of baking bread.

A few weeks out, we make a stop at the island of Akutan. There's a bar, and we all — except Buddy — head for it.

Outside, it looks more like a warehouse than anything. Inside, it's dark with sixties-style paneling and linoleum. The plywood-topped tables are empty, except for the carved names of past guests. We each grab a stool at the faux marble bar, and the bartender comes right over. One by one, he asks us what we'd like.

"Scotch," from Hank.

"Gin and tonic," requests John.

My turn. "I'd like Bailey's and Bushmill's. On ice. Please." I use 'please' carefully to make up for the lack of manners of my crewmates.

Joey orders, "Coors."

Lastly, Gary says, "Scotch."

We sit in blithe anticipation, watching the bartender reach down without moving from his spot. He pulls out five cans of Budweiser, pops their tops, and slams one down in front of each of us. We look at him, then turn to each other for confirmation of our confusion, then back at the bartender, searching for an explanation. He laughs. "What... are you kidding? We have Budweiser. That's all."

Whereever do people get their sense of humor? We drink our beer with less mirth, though still glad for the change of scenery.

When I'm about halfway through my Bud, I walk to the phone in the hall near the bathrooms to call home. Mom picks up on the other end and I know something is wrong immediately. Her tone is overly cheerful. At first, in her typical reluctance to worry others, she's silent on the matter, but I persist.

"Everything is okay," she insists, as my radar zooms in.

"What? What happened? Is everyone alright?"

"He's fine now, but your dad had a stroke. He's recovering in the hospital."

Bam! My heart and stomach collide.

"When?"

"Two days ago. He went to the hospital in town, but they transferred him up to Portland."

"Is he okay?" I ask, even though she's answered the question. But my mind conjures a blank while it processes. "Will it affect his diabetes? Will it make it worse?"

"They say he'll be fine. He has a long recovery ahead, but it should be complete."

"Why didn't anyone tell me? You could have called by marine operator."

"I didn't want you to worry. You know your dad wouldn't want you to come home for this, and I thought it would only distract you."

"Isn't that what family is for? Aren't we supposed to worry about each other? What if he died?"

Quiet on the line.

"I can't get home from here, Mom. I'll fly home as soon as we get back to Dutch." My eyes are stinging so I close them, willing the tears away.

"Don't come home. You'll see him when you're done up there. He'll be fine."

I don't trust that he'll be okay. But on an island in the middle of the Aleutians, there's nothing I can do. I'm scared as I realize for the first time how isolated I am. Thousands of miles of water lie between my father and me. Whatever was I thinking? Anyone could drop dead and here I am – stuck on an island in the middle of literal nowhere with a bunch of assholes, drinking beer in a bar.

"How are things up there?" she tries to change the topic.

"Everything's fine, Mom. Everything's fine."

I let my shipmates know what's happened. They mumble sorrys, and they voice hope for his recovery. After a few minutes, Hank leaves because he's got work to do, and the rest of us soon follow. We need to return to the fishing grounds.

Back on board, I pass the inside ladder to the bridge. Without the engine running, I can hear the conversation above. I catch the "she" word and stop, then climb onto the second step of the ladder — close enough to eavesdrop invisibly. If someone comes from either direction, I can start moving up as though I was already in motion. I feel like a child lying on my belly at the top of the stairs, straining to hear my parents' voices, trying to catch a glimpse of adult life.

Buddy says to Hank, "I won't put up with a cry-baby on board. She'd better have her shit together."

"There's nothing we can do about her except wait and see."

I quietly step down from my perch and head for my quarters. Furious at Buddy's lack of sensitivity, I'm determined to act as though nothing has happened. I recall Dad's admonition to me as a child to "blow your nose and wash your face with cold water," whenever tears escaped my little girl eyes. I do exactly that.

We've switched from fishing Pollock for the Russians, to

fishing true cod for an American processing boat. The fish need to be bled on board our boat before they're transferred to the processor. We fill the cod-end to capacity on almost every tow. That means tons and tons of fish that need bleeding. I offer to go on deck to help, and my offer is accepted. I'm excited about a chance to work alongside the guys, perhaps find camaraderie. Plus, I'll get fresh air and a change of scene from the tiny galley I feel imprisoned in. Those twenty-five square feet slowly suck my spirit, out through the bottoms of my feet.

I use a set of rain gear that the boat carries as extra. It's too big. I roll cuffs into the sleeves and pants, hiking the Grundens' suspenders as high as I can get them without them clawing my crotch. A couple of pairs of socks make the boots more manageable.

On the deck, I'm up to my knees in slippery cod. Their perfectly round black eyes stare out at everything and nothing. One by one, I slit their throats with a stainless steel knife, then throw them into a bin. Repeat. Hour after hour of slicing throats. And though I'm feeling more like a part of the crew, my shipmates don't seem to agree; they never change their distant demeanor. I remain an outsider.

Fish after fish become a meditation of sorts. A mantra. The mindless activity takes me back to childhood...

It was the summer between my first and second grades and my family had recently moved to Sayville, NY. It was a newly built neighborhood, and the storm drains, designed to collect rain and snowmelt and move it to the sump, are unsullied.

My brothers and their friends find joy in opening the manhole covers and exploring the tunnel-world beneath the streets. Every afternoon, it's the same. They collect in a huddle and plan their route for the day. Will they go right or left? Down the new tunnel they'd found yesterday, or continue on to the end of the current tunnel? In the background, I always listen quietly. Even a peep out of me will bring about a forced march home, banished. I'm excluded the moment they start down the hole, but I want to hang around as much as I can, breathing in their adventure and their boy-ness.

It's July and the hottest day of summer so far. There stand my brothers and Joey Williams, waiting for the rest of the gang. I ask, like I do every day. "Please, can I go with you? I'll stay quiet and won't bother anyone. Pleeeeaase?"

"Okay." from Michael, the oldest. I'm stunned at first, then thrilled. My thoughts race, I getta go! I really getta go! I'll show them! I'll be brave and they won't have to wait for me because I'll be fast and strong. They'll see! At the same time, there's this trickle of panic in the back of my belly, a sliver of yellow fear that maybe I can't keep up. But I shut it down as I see the Butler boys running barefoot down the street.

The boys form their usual group on the concrete driveway, making a half circle so they can see Mike and me facing each other while I receive instructions.

Mike continues, "...but you have to be dressed for it."

"What do I wear?"

"Well, it's really cold down there. You'll be surprised. It doesn't get sun or air or anything, so you have to dress like it's winter."

My adoring gaze is on him, taking in every syllable.

"You need to put on long pants, but... " He draws it out, then adds in a blurt, "Long-johns first."

"I don't have long-johns."

Pat to the rescue: "You can use mine. They're in one of my drawers."

I'm amazed at this sudden and radical inclusion and don't think back on the times they'd been down before, shirtless.

"You need to put on as many shirts as you can fit, then a sweater and a winter coat. Didn't forget a hat and mittens. But hurry up, we can't wait all day for you."

"I can do that!"

My dirty, bare summer feet carry me as fast as they can, into the house. Mom doesn't know what the boys are doing, and even though not a word was spoken about it, I know I'm sworn to silence. I go to my brothers' room and find Pat's long johns, stuffed far into the back of his bottom drawer. I race back to my room and grab shirts, pants, and a coat out of the drawers and closet. I'm stumped about gloves and a hat. But I remember that when we'd moved in, Mom put boxes in the front hall closet marked "winter." I race down the stairs dressed in off-white, waffle patterned long johns and two shirts. I tear open the closet door and see the box. I rip the cardboard corner in my hurry to open it, and rummage through, finding mittens and a U-Haul orange, woolen watch cap.

Things don't fit back in after my visit, so I leave them in a hump, spilling over the sides of the box, and then slam the door shut. I run back up the stairs to the room I share with my little sister, arriving as my mother reaches the foot of the steps.

"What's going on? Where are your brothers, and why aren't you with them?"

"They're outside. I'm going out in a sec."

"All right, then. Have fun. Don't be late for supper."

I finish dressing with pants, socks and shoes and tiptoe down the stairs. With so many layers under my pants, I can barely bend my knees. My arms are outstretched because my elbows are so fully engulfed in winter clothing. Hat on, one brown and one red mis-sized mitten adorning my hands, I reach the front door and, as gently as I can, push it open. I hold onto it as it closes so it won't slam; one or more of us kids yanking the door open violently has already mangled the closer. Once it's shut, I hobble down the concrete path along the front of the house to see my brothers standing in the street with their friends, already opening the manhole cover. I stop, confused, they were gonna wait for me. There they stand, wearing shorts and no shirts, flashlights at the ready. Joey turns and sees me and elbows brother Bob, a wide grin coming to his chubby face. Bob looks up and, within seconds, they're all looking my way, laughing and pointing. Michael bends over, he's laughing so hard.

I turn and go back into the house, up the stairs to my room. I stand on my bed and peek out the window as the last of them disappears down the drainpipe, leaving the manhole cover slightly ajar.

The fishing is good, and we can't keep up with the onslaught of cod on the deck. I need to cook and the guys need to sleep.

Buddy hires a kid from the processor to bleed fish at a hundred bucks a day – that's ten dollars more than he's paying me. I'm dumbfounded. Humiliated. I swear to myself that I will never bleed another fish. I'll never come back to this fucking boat.

Back in the galley, I cut myself - a little slice from the pointer finger of my left hand. I grab a Band-Aid, put it on, and start bawling. I am tired of being alone. I miss knowing where I stand and what's expected of me. Remembering Buddy's 'no babies on board' motto, I go to my room. Lying on the hard deck with the engine muffling the sound, I cry until my stomach cramps.

CHAPTER EIGHTEEN

Bering Sea

The weather picks up again, and radio chatter warns of a storm, headed our way. We bounce over to the leeward side of Unmak Island. The anchor goes down and the auxiliary power comes on. We take our turns on watch while everyone else sleeps. Mine is the first watch. On the bridge, Buddy stands too close and gives me a brief explanation of my duties. His brown eyes are dull as they meet mine, and I know he's done flirting with me.

"There's not much to do – just keep an eye out once in awhile. Watch a movie if you want, but come up to the bridge every half hour or so to check around. If you hear any changes to the noise of the generator, wake Hank up."

I can smell him. The scent reminds me of hay - sweet and earthy, but a bit on the decaying side.

He points toward a steady column of smoke, rising over a high spot on the barren island. "That's the volcano, over there – Okmok. See the steam coming up? It's active, one of the most active volcanoes in the Islands. We were close when it went off a few years ago. Messed with our air filters, and we could smell the sulfur in the air. The sky turned brownish yellow. Now it's mostly quiet because it's building up for another blow. If that happens today, you can wake me up, but that's the only reason you can wake me."

Over the next few hours, the wind picks up even more, howling at more than 100 knots. Demon-sounds scream and rattle the rigging. It's blowing so hard that the wind completely flattens the water, the surface laced with a mantilla of white streaks and lather that cling and swirl across the surface. I walk out of the house and feel the energy of that wind. It's like electricity through my core, tingling away. I peek my head around the house. Tiny darts of ice freckle my face and I am pushed back. Huddled on the deck near a ledge is a small bird, shaking. I reach out, but withdraw. He'll find his way when it calms.

By the second day of not fishing, everyone is rested, but the wind continues to wail. The guys are watching a movie, and I decide it would be good to join them. I come from my room and out to the galley, which doubles as the entertainment center.

They're sitting in a semi-circle around the table, focused so entirely on the video that they don't notice me walk in. I look at the screen to see a man with two large breasted women – one sitting on his face, the other astride his pelvis. Hank looks up at me and, without changing his vacuous expression, returns his attention to the screen. The shame of my invisibility bursts inside my chest and rises up to push against the inside of my skull. I continue moving, and make my way to the wheelhouse.

Lost in the tall, swiveled captain's chair, I'm that tiny bird in the lee of this storm. I look out toward the simmering volcano on Unmak and smolder against the inconsideration of my shipmates. The transgressions of the captain and crew stab at my heart while the slights, sexist remarks, and sexual innuendos rumble in my belly.

With time, my thoughts wander home, to Dad. Is he still in the hospital? Are there tubes sticking out of him and are nurses poking him with needles? Is he alone?

I wonder what it is that connects me to him? It isn't words or moments spent together - there have been too few of them. But there's a string that begins midway between my heart and my gut, and it flies on the tail of a crow, right to him. It's like monofilament made of titanium - invisible but unbreakable. But it's a one-way line that I've tried severing with knives of words and actions. But the blades turn to ash.

I watch the continuous stream of smoke escaping Okmok Caldera, barely detectable against the backdrop of clouds. I can almost feel the hot magma building beneath the surface, waiting for enough pressure to erupt.

That line in my center anchors itself, and memories begin to tug.

...the way he'd load us all into his yellow Buick Electra in the snow and make fishtails, and the exhilarating terror.

...curling up to him in our Boston Whaler as we flew across the waves of Long Island Sound, and the safety of him surrounding me.

...and the shame of getting caught stealing those hip-hugger denim jeans from The Village Cargo when I was eleven.

If I were to lose him now, there would be so much left unsaid. I'm aware that, even now, there is so much we'll never share.

Alternately, I think of Dad's meanness - the streak that runs through him that confounds me.

I must have been eight or so. It was moments before 5:00 on a Wednesday in our house. We kids were all home because if we were late the rule was we did the dishes. Six kids between the ages of two and ten, we were full of the energy of a tornado. LeRoy, our English Springer Spaniel, was bouncing around from kid to kid, trying to find attention. Margaret and I were fighting over who sat next to Dad. It was a frequent argument. I was the big sister, so it was clearly my place, but she thought she should get it. We were both standing at the table, side by side, pushing against each other as hard as we could. Our little bodies shoved with all the determination of seven and eight year olds, a battle to the death for a twenty-minute prize. Foot against foot, bony shoulder rubbing against bony shoulder, mine a bit higher. We moved back to back to try to gain traction. Fists tight, jaws clamped and eyes squinting to find every last ounce of available strength. She was surprisingly strong, but I was edging her out, feeling victorious. Just as I was sure to win, she turned to the table and grabbed the plate, then put it to her face. She stuck her tongue out and used every one of her tiny taste buds to transfer her germs to it. Outsmarted by a seven-year-old.

"You can't do that! No fair! That's not fair!" I screamed.

"It's mine now!"

We'd been so loud we hadn't heard our father come in.

"What the hell is going on here?"

Everyone stopped, and the house fell silent. Margaret dropped her arm and held the plate to her side.

"I said what's going on?"

Margaret and I both started talking at once. 'She pushed me.' 'She started it.'

"Shaddup," he yelled. When he knew he had our attention he looked back and forth between my sister and me. "What happened?"

I felt his nearness, the way he had of taking me over. The only thing that existed in the universe was him, and he vacuumed my spirit.

Silence.

"Why were you two fighting? Huh? Margaret, what are you doing with that plate?"

In an act of great courage, she told the truth. "I licked it."

Dad reached forward and grabbed the plate. He extended it over her head and jerked a pile of potatoes onto it. We turned to the table and watched as he forked a piece of meatloaf on, then peas. Two green balls fell off the plate and rolled across the floor. He handed the meal to her, but she didn't take it. He pushed it to her chest.

"Take it," he barked. "If you're going to act like a dog, you can eat with the dog."

We all looked at him. All of us except Margaret, who looked at the peas on the floor. Dad's eyes did not veer from her. "I said go. Back with LeRoy. You're eating with him tonight." The silence did not let up as she took the plate and walked back to where the animals ate.

His eyes found my eyes and he said, "One word from you and you'll join her."

I didn't even look at Mom - I knew she didn't see.

Throughout dinner, I thought of my sister back there. I wanted to grab my plate, get up, and join her. I wanted us all to stand up and leave the table. But I sat and ate my meal because I knew that if I didn't, it would be waiting for me in the morning.

Dinner was silent, and the coveted place next to our dad remained empty. I swore that I hated him, but still, I was swallowed up in wanting his love. Margaret never fought for that spot again, and it never meant the same to me.

Still, his approval is everything to me. Just a moment of his attention makes me yearn for more. Maybe it's the way it feels like I'm the only one on the planet when he pays attention to me that makes me need him so.

I move my hands to the wooden ship's wheel and try to spin it, but without forward momentum it doesn't budge against the weight of the water.

Epiphany hits. This is my attempt to know my father. I'd thought that if I could do this one thing that he and my brothers did, if I could fish, I might know his heart. I'm Dorothy in the *Wizard of Oz*, traveling far into another world to find my way home. Except there is no Wizard, and I don't know where home is.

I climb nimbly down the ladder and continue past the galley table without a glance. I head straight for my quarters, grab a bottle of Crown Royal from the drawer and settle in. My back to the bulkhead, I drink in gulps, straight from the bottle. The fire consumes my mouth and my throat, but the physical pain of the burn gives me an opportunity to focus on something other than the pain in my heart.

CHAPTER NINETEEN

Bering Sea

When I wake, more than half the bottle is gone. My stomach is a maze with no exit. It contains a family of hungry mice scurrying to find their way out. My mouth is a web of in-dissolvable cotton candy, and the sugar is replaced with vinegar and toe jam. The shame returns, or maybe it never left.

I get up, take a shower and put on my last set of clean clothes.

The storm starts to pass, but another — this one larger than the last ˆ is headed our way. We're short on supplies and Buddy decides to use the brief window to run into Dutch. We leave the shelter of the bay.

Although the wind has laid down, the seas haven't subsided, and the expected hurricane force storm is following in the distance, sending its warning pulses out in advance. We're getting thrown around. Hard. Buddy yells down, "Get me some coffee up here!" I go up the ladder to the bridge and grab his special mug. He has a ceramic mug that never, and I mean never, gets washed. Except once.

When I'd come on board, his cup was so full of layered coffee stains, I wouldn't have known it was off-white from looking at the inside. I grabbed a box of baking soda and scrubbed until it shined. When I returned it to him, sparkling and full of coffee, he acted like I'd thrown insults at his dead grandmother; in turn he got angry and then acted as if he'd lost something precious.

"What did you do?"

I was confused, so I said the obvious "I cleaned your coffee cup. Better, huh?"

"That cup has never been washed. It's supposed to be that way. It'll taste like soap for months. Two things you need to know. I want my coffee just below boiling, and I want a seasoned cup. Don't clean it again. You can rinse it with water."

Thanks for the info. I haven't repeated the mistake, and now it looks like it did before I cleaned it.

Back in the galley, my emotions have cycled around and now they're a cyclone of anger. I pull the stainless steel carafe out from behind the bungee cord that holds it in place at the same time one of those beam seas smashes against the boat. I'm flown toward the counter as the pot of hot coffee sloshes out of the pot. The counter stops me with a jolt, but the coffee keeps moving up and out of the pot, onto the soft skin of my belly.

You are not going to scream. You are not going to yell.

I move with the next lunge of the ship and grab the counter as I drop the metal pot into the sink. I lean over so layers of hot shirts aren't resting against my skin, and unbutton, then unzip, my jeans. My pants undone and peeled away from the reddening skin, I grab a cloth and put it in a bowl. I turn to the freezer and open it to grab a tray of ice at the moment the boat hits the nadir of the current wave. I close and latch the door and then, twisting the mold of ice over the bowl, I turn the water off and press the cold cloth to my tummy, water dripping out over my pants and onto the deck. I repeat the process, but it's clear that no amount of water will stop the blisters from forming.

My inside voice says 'wash your face with cold water.' Out loud I say, "Suck it up."

Buddy yells from the bridge for his coffee. I go to the bottom of the ladder and in my calmest, loudest voice say, "I spilled it. I'm putting a fresh pot on."

I grab a bag of frozen peas and put it on my stomach. I go to my room and change into dirty sweat pants and, walking like a crab, return to the galley to make the fresh pot.

Swaying and lunging back and forth with the movement of the waves, I bring Buddy his half-full cup.

I say, "When I spilled the coffee, I was in the way. I've got a good burn that looks like it'll blister. Probably should see someone when we hit Dutch."

"Let me see."

His insults and meanness bring courage to my lips. "I'm not pulling my pants down for you. Trust me – it's bad."

"Make sure you ice it," he says in an attempt to regain control.

"Already started," I reply as I turn toward the ladder.

He radios ahead to set an appointment for me.

By the time we arrive in port, it's occurred to me that this could be my ticket out of here. My way to get home to see Dad without saying it's about Dad. If the burn is bad enough, there won't be any shame in leaving. They'll say it's a bad idea to go back out. I begin to think about how good it will be to see everyone. My heart pulls a wad of hope inward, and it settles. I'm convinced they'll send me home.

At the clinic, the doctor examines me and tells me it's a bad burn, but it shouldn't keep me from working. He gives me Silvadene ointment, in case it starts to get infected.

"You mean I can go back to work? What if it gets worse?"

"You'll be fine," he says. 'Buck up,' I hear.

I return to the boat, knowing that I can't possibly make it through another month or more. My heart was set on the doctor proclaiming me unfit-for-duty.

Too chicken-shit to quit — too scared to tell Buddy what I think of him, his boat and his crew, I lie. I tell him that the burn is fine, but that I bruised a kidney when I hit the table. I need to go home.

For dinner on my last night, I cook liver and onions. Some people actually like the stuff. Me? I can't stand the thought of eating it.

I grab the cast iron skillet from the cabinet, and turn the range to medium-high heat, squirting oil in. After that heats up, I throw in thinly sliced onions, stirring and cooking them to a deep, golden brown. The smell is like a light, warm quilt covering everything in the galley. It's comforting, like going into the kitchen of a fat, German grandma.

For the last few minutes, I sweep the onions to the side of the pan and, one by one, add the thin, blood-brown slabs of liver. The scent creates a direct path to my childhood.

I was six, and my dad was cooking liver and onions - one of his favorite dishes. Every time he cooked this wretched meal, everyone in the house scattered.

This day, I made a decision with my child-brain. I'd eat liver and onions.

When it was all cooked and he sat down at the table, I quietly walked over. "Daddy, could I please try some?"

That mischievous glint he would get varnished his eyes. "Sure, Sha," he said. He cut a teensy piece from the edge. He picked it up with his fork and extended the gift to me.

I took the morsel, and it was everything I expected it to be. On my tongue, it felt soft and fiberless, like a dense sponge made of mashed mushrooms. And, if taste had a color? It would have been grayish brown, tinged with mold-green .

The liver sat in the middle of my tongue while I decided what to do with it. I wanted to open my mouth to let the air take some of the taste away. Instead, I swallowed it whole. The front part of my tongue pushed up against the roof of my mouth, forcing the thing toward the back, then down toward my stomach. The foul flavor clung to my tongue.

"Mmm...I like it." I sat down at the long, heavy wooden table in the seat to his right. The chair, while it swallowed me, gave me a feeling of safety and comfort. It was only the two of us in the kitchen, but I could hear the sound of cartoons coming from the playroom where two of my brothers and my sister were watching TV.

To his credit, he didn't blink an eye. He cut up another piece, and we sat in silence, sharing liver and onions. And the silence was okay with me. I glowed with my father's attention, and basked in the knowledge that my dad and I shared this thing that was ours, and ours alone. In that one vile meal lived father and daughter and pain and love and longing. They all mashed up together in that little girl heart of mine.

Buddy's liver is done — too done. I've let my thoughts wander over-long, but what the hell — it's liver and onions, and it's my second-to-last meal. I'll be on my way to the airport after breakfast tomorrow. I splash oil right on top.

No goodbyes. I leave the boat after I've cleaned up from breakfast and get a cab to the airport. It's packed with every fisherman who was supposed to get off during the past week of storms, and is ten times as full as when I'd flown in. Hundreds of guys in beards and sweats, standing, sitting in chairs, or lying on bags, many of them sleeping.

I walk up to the ticket counter. The brunette behind the tall desk looks at me with a face that's stoically ready for combat.

"Hi. Portland, please," in my most innocent voice.

"Sorry, ma'am. Flights are booked. We have one leaving soon, but nothing's taken off since Friday, so it's full. We can get you a ticket for Wednesday, but with the way the weather's been, there's no guarantee."

"Wednesday's three days from now," I whine, as if she doesn't know. My skin is now tingling with fear.

"Sometimes that happens," she says. Like a kindergarten teacher, placating a student who has anxiety about leaving her mother. "The weather's been bad. It looks like we have a window for the next flight, but there's another front headed our way."

"But I can't wait three days!"

"Well, there's nothing I can do about that. I'm terribly sorry."

She must know there's not one room available on the island. I look frantically around the airport at the grunged out fishermen. She can't leave me here. Tears don't come, but my eyes water as I plead: "Look, my dad's had a stroke, I got off a fishing boat, and I need to get home. Isn't there something you can do?"

She looks at me and then around the airport as I had. "Let me see." She types into her keyboard and says quietly, as a secret shared between us, "I've got you through to Seattle. You can board in an hour and you'll be on standby from there."

"Thank you. I don't know what to say. Thank you, thank you."

CHAPTER TWENTY

Newport, Oregon

The airline doesn't carry Crown Royal, so my homeward companions are 1.7 ounce bottles of cheap whiskey. By the time I reach the Portland Airport, I'm in a fog. I throw my duffel into the trunk of my brother's aging brown, Fiat Spider. He says Dad's doing well, but that he has trouble walking. He's slower and, well... older. I wake as we pull up to my folks' house. Its opulence is lost on me these days. My sister is married so I have the west wing to myself - two bedrooms with two bathrooms and matching fireplaces backed up to each other. The door to my side of the house is separated by a door to the rest of the house. There's a lock on that door that I heard kept a crazy wife locked away. I throw myself into the wooden posted, full-sized bed that I've had since I was ten, without showering.

Next day, I find my father making oatmeal at the kitchen counter. The sparkle's gone from his eyes, but there's a lightness that takes them over when he sees me.

"Hi, Sha."

"Heya Poppolo. How ya feeling?"

"Good. I'm walking better than I was. Your mom won't let me use my electrical tools, but I'm getting better all the time." Is this my father? Even if he did let Mom tell him what he can and can't do, he'd never admit to it. "Why are you home?" he continues, "What happened? I thought you were up there for a few more months."

Gawd, I hate being a failure, and quitters are failures. It's not so bad when I keep it to myself, but saying it out loud, to him, makes it sting. I think about lying, but any lie I can think of makes me look even worse. I give him a half-truth.

"They were a bunch of jerks, Dad. I hated it up there."

He barely pauses before saying, "Well, something will come up." His eyes look to the door, then back to me. His jaw wrinkles from side to side, almost imperceptibly.

These are our conversations. Straight. To the point. But there's a whole planet hidden beneath the surface. His disappointment turns in my stomach like a beached starfish.

I stay in my old room at my folks' house while I decide what to do next. Fishing wasn't so bad, I tell myself. I was getting the hang of cooking, and liked the schedule – a few months at work, then a few months off. Phil was great. If I could combine Phil's nature and the Mariner's fish, life would be perfect.

I'm at the house, contemplating my options while I'm chopping onions for dinner. Dad comes in through the back door, dressed in his coveralls. I can tell immediately he needs to ingest something with loads of sugar. He's moving slowly, and his eyes are glazed and unfocused.

Constantly on the alert for a diabetic meltdown, we always have orange juice in the freezer. The sugar in the juice gives his blood the glucose it needs, fast.

"Hey Poppolo — how about a glass of orange juice?" I saunter over to the freezer to grab a can. I'm upbeat, calm, and cool as I try to sneak it by like it's a regular question.

"I don't need any gawdamned orange juice — I want iced tea."

Shit. Combat mode. For my dad, it's one of the less charming side effects of a diabetic reaction.

I grab the can out of the freezer and head for the sink, tearing at the plastic-tab closure. "Wow, that sounds great. Why don't you make tea and I'll make OJ, in case you want it later." Taking a spoon, I dig out about a third of the concentrate and add hot water to melt it. I use a fork to mash it together, then pour cold water on top to make it palatable. I turn around and see Dad standing in front of the refrigerator door as he might stand in front of a urinal. And that's exactly what he's using it for. I put the juice down and yell. "Dad! Quit that right now!"

His hand drops from the refrigerator door and he crumples to the ground.

I don't stop to check on him on my way to the phone — I know exactly what's happening, and I can't help him. The knowledge doesn't keep the tears from forming or my hands from shaking as I pick up the phone. Nor does it keep my voice from faltering on the first try.

"I...I..." I hear my voice, or rather feel the words trying to come out. I try again. "I..I'm at 380 SE Penter Lane. My Dad's having a diabetic attack and needs an ambulance. He's collapsed."

"Yes, ma'am. What's your name?"

I tell them.

"Hold, please."

I look over to my father, lying on the brown and beige, short-napped carpet. His eyes are closed, but I see movement in his chest. I'm afraid if I let the phone down to check, the operator will come back on line and things will be held up. I hold and watch.

Within seconds, the woman is back on the line. "All right, Miss, we have an ambulance on the way. I need you to stay with me until they arrive. Do not leave the phone."

I reach the cord as far as I can and sit on the floor near my father while we wait for the ambulance. I take a chance and let my phone hand stray from my ear while I reach and bring his slack hand toward me. I hold it while I look at his face. His skin sags like a partially deflated Mylar balloon.

After a few minutes, I hear the siren. Letting go of the phone and his hand, I get up and run to the door to guide the EMTs into the kitchen.

A man enters, dressed in a white shirt and black — or maybe they're blue — pants, carrying a large, red box. A man and woman follow close behind with a stretcher between them. One of them picks up the telephone, briefly acknowledges their arrival on the scene, then hangs up. The other two shake Dad, yell at him, talk on the radio, then yell and shake some more. "Are you all right? Are you all right?"

The third medic and I stand to the side. Brad, says his name tag. I smell his aftershave — spices and earth. I watch the action on the floor intently as he asks me questions.

'What happened? How old is he? Do you know how much insulin he's had today?'

'He had a diabetic attack. He collapsed. I called you. He's 59. I don't know how much insulin.'

My arms cross my chest, clutching every ounce of fear inside. Wanting to be invulnerable.

An EMT takes a needle out and I turn my head. Brad steps forward and whispers with one of the others — the one not holding a needle. He returns. "We'll take him to the hospital. You can ride along or follow in another car."

A sequence of logistical thoughts brings me to a conclusion. How is it that logic can exist in this rattled brain? That's what my father says, "If you had a brain it would rattle." It's rattling now, Dad.

"I'll meet you there."

A few minutes later, he's lying on the stretcher, beginning to regain consciousness. He gazes at me through rheumy eyes with a sadness I've never seen before. No words. I smile and touch the blanket that covers his arm.

Before I leave, I call Mom at work.

"Dad's had a reaction. He's in the ambulance."

"I'll meet you at the ER."

Words. They say what's going on, but they don't say what's going on. Missing is the question: How bad is it this time?

Dad spends the night in the hospital. His rapid rises and plunges in blood sugar are becoming more frequent, but this one was plain scary.

CHAPTER TWENTY-ONE

Newport, Oregon

After a night out drinking, I'm at home in my parents' house. I've been kicked out of the Pip Tide, and, worse yet, the Bay Haven. That's never happened before. Something about yelling at the bartender. At least I took a cab home. I mean... that was the right thing to do. I didn't drink and drive, so I can't be that bad. Or, maybe I am. Maybe I do have a problem. I saw my friend, Linda, last week. She quit drinking. Maybe I should do the same. I admit to myself that I've tried to quit many times. I've made promises to myself to stop drinking that were sometimes kept for only hours. Maybe I really am an alcoholic.

It's one a.m. and the house is quiet. I turn on the television and sit on the brown leather sofa to douse myself in the mindless drivel of an animated screen. I surf through reruns of "Dragnet," and "Starsky & Hutch," interrupted by furniture commercials with Tom Peterson and his flat-top haircut. He's the only person I know with that hairstyle – other than Dad. Marine-style. A quarter inch of hair standing at full salute, sides clipped close. Tom is knocking irritatingly against the inside of the screen. "Wake up! Wake up!" Trying to get me to buy a new TV. I change the channel. The idea that I'm an alcoholic won't let go of me, as if it's the first time the possibility has ever occurred to me. I shut it down. Again.

I land on a station with a man in a suit, standing at a pulpit. He says his ministry has saved countless people from a fate worse than death – living in poverty of spirit. My hand pauses on the channel control. Isn't that me? Isn't my spirit suffering a crisis? He talks about those who've been healed of moral decrepitude. Isn't that me? Am I not a bad person? A female Dorian Gray, trying desperately to hide my fears and deficits, constantly afraid I'll be found out for who I am?

A call can't hurt, can it? I mean they can't convert me over the phone, right? I'm willing to do almost anything to rid myself of the tornado in my head. Believing in God is a stretch, but I could pretend. Maybe they can help me with one of those treatment programs.

I call the 800-number on the screen and turn down the television's volume. A woman answers.

"Praise Jesus, I'm Kathy, who's this?"

"Uh, Theresa."

"Theresa! God bless you. How much would you like to donate to our ministry?" Her southern drawl sounds affected to me.

"I'm sorry, I can't give you anything. I...I was hoping maybe somebody there could, could..."

"What seems to be the problem, dear?"

"Well, um... I want to go into treatment for alcoholics and I don't have money. All the people you help, I thought maybe you could help me?"

"Oh, I aaam sorry, sweetie, but this line only takes contributions. We don't really assist people like tha-at."

"Oh. Then could you maybe tell me who to call?"

"Now that is a good question, and I do wish there was something I could do, but unless you want to donate, I can't help. Try your local church."

Click.

I continue to hold the phone next to my ear. It's like a stoplight has turned yellow; I've taken my foot off the gas, but haven't moved it to the brake. I asked for help and she hung up on me. It doesn't make sense. I mean, someone's desperate like that, you at least say something. You at least try.

Like a snake, humiliation wraps itself around my core and squeezes. All screwed up from my belly to my throat, I get up and slither unsteadily back to the bedroom that I call mine.

I sit cross-legged on the bed. I look around at my accumulated life and turn my eyes to the teapot on the mantle of the fireplace. My father purchased it for his mother while he was in the Korean War. He gave it to me when she died. White porcelain with dainty pink flowers, gold stems and green leaves, it brings a smile to my heart when I see it. Tonight, thinking of my father and grandmother brings shame. I go to the closet and grab the half-full bottle of vodka stashed there.

Morning slams into me like a log truck gearing down on a gravel road. Even though the direct sun won't hit this side of the house until after noon, I'm sure the diffuse light will burn my eyes out. I close them gently and the fine grit that's accumulated on the insides of the lids scrapes against my eyeballs. I squeeze the lids lightly, trying to force a cleansing tear or two. Nothing. I lie there and remember the call from the night before, and get pissed-off again that a charlatan has duped me. But now that it's come up, treatment seems my only answer, and I have no idea where I can get the kind of money I need for it.

Shifting delicately to the nearest end of the bed, I hesitate before sliding my legs to the edge. I gently move them over the side and drop my feet down to the floor at the same time as I lift my upper body to a sitting position, using my right hand for balance.

The whirlies hit immediately. I slump back onto the mattress. Within seconds, I jump back up and barely make it to the toilet. There's no time to lift the seat before a foul gush erupts from my stomach — up and out, toward the white porcelain bowl. Most of it hits the target. I make it to my knees before the second onslaught. The cold of the tile seeps through my jeans; I never undressed for bed.

When I'm finished, I lift myself up, grab the trash container, and teeter back into the bedroom.

The room is in shambles. Nothing remains on the bedside stand or the fireplace mantle. The dresser top is empty. Not one surface holds anything except vague outlines of dust. It makes no sense.

Then I see it. My grandmother's teapot. There it lies, partly on the stone hearth, partly on the carpeted floor, its graceful spout decapitated, its body and lid in shards.

I grope my way through to last night, trying to remember what happened. Nothing. I blacked out again.

Tears begin to crawl out my eyes and creep down my cheeks, the first ones scratchy and burning. They come more fluidly then, and soon roll, one after the other, no space between.

Like a river in the spring thaw picks up creeks and streams along the way, tears gather all the pent up anguish in my heart. River gathers detritus – things left in times of drought – gas cans, lawn chairs, forgotten toys. She uproots bushes and trees. She changes the landscape as she travels along, growing and shifting. So it is that my tears pick up the years of hoarded sadness. With breaths alternating shallow to deep, in turns I suffocate and come to the surface for draughts of air. I drop to the floor and pull my legs up to my chest, trying to rebuild the dam I've engineered over the course of my life. But the power of the breach is too great – there's no plaster for the leaks and it's a full river now. Again I gulp for air, and then am pulled back down by the raging current, the river running relentlessly downward, toward the sea.

CHAPTER TWENTY-TWO

Oregon

My parents pay for a stay at Serenity by the Sea. Twenty-eight days later, they meet me inside the front door. Mom hugs me, and then Dad and I have a sideways hug. He moves toward the front door, eager to get out of this place. When we get to their car, he reaches in and pulls out a tan teddy bear. He's holding it by an arm, and I accept it by the butt. Drawing the bear toward me, I curl him in toward my chest. Madonna and Child. Dad's blue eyes seem bluer through a fine film of moisture. Sunshine and clouds, all at once.

It's a soft bear. His hips are perpetually bent into a sitting position. If he could stand, he'd be about a foot tall. Dangling from a narrow bow around his neck is a medallion, a gold heart. I know immediately that his name is Bernard, and he won't ever leave me, nor I him.

We take the two-hour drive home, Mom updating me on what I've missed. Mike's working in Houston, Bob's back up in Dutch. Pat and his wife are living back on Long Island, Margaret and her husband are in Newport, brother Jim and his wife in Eugene. Nothing's changed, but I wonder about fitting back in. Dad quit drinking a few years ago because of his diabetes, but everyone else drinks whenever we get together.

Although welcome at my folks' house, I'm determined to live on my own, like other adults. I find paradise in a white, one bedroom house that looks out onto Yaquina Bay. Sitting at my dining room table I can look out and see the boats coming and going beneath the gracefully-arched Roosevelt-era bridge.

I can't go back to fishing yet because being at sea would keep me from my counseling sessions and support meetings. Plus, although I don't want to live with my parents, it's good to be close to them, especially with Dad's health. I get my old job back at the Pip-Tide as a cocktail waitress. My new, sober friends don't think it's such a good idea, but I need a job and the money's decent.

Instead of drinking on my nights off, I sit in my living room watching movies and eating Ding Dongs. Box after box of disgustingly delicious chocolate cakes with chemical white filling, brimming with high fructose corn syrup. They partially satisfy the sugar-void once filled by alcohol.

On the job, I watch as my coworkers swallow shots of booze from ceramic coffee mugs. Although illegal, the bartenders are generous with their pours until the staggering and slurring become obvious. In my newfound purity, I look on them with pity as they fill their mugs.

I've been back for about four weeks when I start this particular shift. Midway through the night, Kevin, the man I've been flirting with for the past month, comes in. He's groping a woman. They're not in my section, but I can't help looking their way every chance I get. The two of them are having a ripping-good time, slamming shots of tequila, sucking on limes, wincing their eyes, then downing chasers of beer. They head out every half-hour and come back in with sniffly noses. She's prettier than I am, petite and cute. Girlie-cute. Hair done up with spray, perfect lips on a perfect complexion. Fingernails bright red, a couple of matching toes peek out from stiletto sandals that bring her up to about 5'5". As the night wears on, they're practically screwing on the dance floor.

The problem with being sober is that I can't run from myself. Even anger won't pummel my hurt. At the waitress station, I get a shot of Cuervo Gold from Dana, the bartender. Even as I push the empty mug toward him, even as he asks me with higher than usual eyebrows if I'm sure. Even as I smell the liquid and then feel the burn, I know I oughtn't. I really know I oughtn't. But here it is. Here I am. I drink. And I drink some more.

Stumbling the two blocks home after talking Dana out of an eight-ounce Styrofoam cup of tequila, I drink it and relish it. Over and over, I view my brain's video of Kevin fondling that woman, and her fondling back. I make up additional scenes and play those. I get stinking drunk. I get shit-faced. And all the while, I know it's wrong.

But, the next night, I do it again. I drink again and again for a month.

On Memorial Day Saturday, I dress in a short black skirt and low cut, white tank top, and I walk to work, shaky from the night before. On my way, I think about how I really, really am tired of this. About how I miss giving a shit.

At the bar, I stop at the step leading down to my station, the one that holds those white ceramic mugs. It's early, but the band is warming up and the gals that always follow them around are there with the guys that follow them around. Groupies watching groupies. They're making perfect bar noises. Rumble, rumble, whisper, laugh. Repeat. Repeat and repeat again. Louder laughter. Clap at the music and fawn over the band at the appropriate moments. I know this by heart. I live it. As for the station, everything is closer than it was the last time I was in, and I'm suffocating from the stench of the filthy carpet. My heart is beating fast and I'm dizzy. Dana is at the bar, grabbing a bottle from the top shelf in slow motion. I turn and walk back out the door without a word.

Two days later, I return. I know I have to make apologies. Wayne, the manager, is standing on a wide set of stairs that leads up to the gambling room. There's a handrail and his right elbow is set on it. His right leg is one step higher than his left and he's overlooking the bar, the benevolent ruler of this dark world. I walk up to him and he smiles at me like he does. Cheshire cat.

"Hey, Wayne."

"Hi Theresa, how's it going?"

As if nothing had happened.

"Better. And I'm sorry about the other night, but Wayne, I can't work here anymore. I hope you understand. I can't do it." I drip defeat.

"I knew it would happen."

"What?"

"Go home. Take care of yourself. Get well."

CHAPTER TWENTY-THREE

Newport, Oregon

My parents move to a smaller house in Newport. We're within a few miles of each other, and I spend time with them every week. I have dinner with the two of them, or go shopping with Dad, though he frustrates me. Often, he asks my opinion on food, but never listens to it. A normal scenario goes like this:

Ring, ring.

"Hello."

"Hey Sha, why don't you come on over for dinner?"

"Sure, Dad. What are you making?"

"I'm thinking about a sirloin roast. How would you cook it?"

I'm flattered that he asks my opinion. Something new since my job on the *Mariner*.

"Well, usually that's done dry, in the oven, maybe some spices rubbed on top." I say this with all the authority bestowed upon me in my months of experience.

"Sounds good. I think I'll cut it up and make a stew. Sound good?"

He gets me every time.

"Yeah, Dad. Sounds good."

Today, I'm in the neighborhood, and stop to say hi.

I park next to his pickup and get out. Dad's coming out the front door.

"Hey Poppolo, what's up?"

He's got his keys in his hand, heading toward the garage. "I thought I'd head down to the LNG plant."

That means one thing: Salmon fishing.

"Are they running? It seems early."

"I guess I'll find out."

"Want some company?"

He seems alone and at odds with his post-stroke lifestyle. He can't use machinery and can't go out on his drift boat. Mom's at work during the day and the house is quiet. I hate sport fishing, and I don't like salmon fishing, but I dislike seeing Dad in a funk even more.

"Sure," he says, "Come along."

The drive to the green tank that holds liquid natural gas takes about ten minutes. The tank sits next to the bay, and has a berm of jetty-sized rocks that keep the man-made peninsula from eroding back to its natural shoreline. Dad parks the truck and grabs his fishing pole, and I grab the tackle box. We walk down the rumpled rock faces to the boulder closest to the water. There are no other fishermen around, which answers the question of whether the fish are running. But he wants to fish. He says it isn't called catching.

We spend a few hours on the rock, the low winter sun warming us, him with his pole, casting, reeling, casting. Both of us are quiet. I don't know why we have nothing to say and, when we do, we often disagree. Like the food thing. Or how fast to drive, or where to set the side-view mirrors.

It's not like having the television on to The News or a John Wayne movie. Those times it's best to keep quiet to avoid the "Shaddup" that comes from disturbing his programs. Now, we're quiet because we have nothing to say, and, if I did talk, he might give a warning not to scare the fish, but I think we both know there are no fish today. I wonder why he's here as I gaze out to the water that I've come to know in her many faces. But I notice that the gray tones his skin's taken on lately have disappeared in the breeze, the salt and the sun. He's better, I tell myself.

CHAPTER TWENTY-FOUR

Newport, Oregon

I stand inside the door of the hospital room. The smell of sickness and antiseptic is heavier here than it was in the corridor. Added to it is the scent of stargazer lilies, which ought to be outlawed in hospitals. Their uber-sweet smell is as powerful as a thousand roses, piled up and decaying. It glazes the insides of my nose, a veneer of sickness and death.

It's a two-bed room, and the curtain to the closest bed is pulled shut. Dad's bed is, thankfully, nearest the window; beds near the door are so pathetically public. I walk past the faded blue cotton drape to reach him. He's sleeping, and I see him at peace.

In this instant, his fierceness is gone. His eyes are closed and his breathing's slow and depthless. I'm a benevolent thief, stealing a sliver of time that does not belong to me. The white coverlet rises and falls, its thick, square weave making a pattern of a million exact replicas of angular hills and valleys, reaching out to the east, the south, the west, and the north. The palest green cotton hospital gown peeks out the top.

All of that life, all of those dreams, all of that anger and power and love, reduced to a solitary man who depends on an uninterrupted flow of air to survive.

A waterfall of calm pools at the top of my head and flows down, washing away the fear and confusion, leaving behind an immense well of love. Sadness at his mortality mingles with a feeling of personal strength. There is balance in the room.

He stirs.

"Hey Poppolo," I whisper.

He opens his eyes and, for a heartbeat, does not recognize me. Then a smile comes into his eyes and forms faintly on his dry, ashen lips. I put my hand on his arm, and bend to him with a cheek kiss. Light as a butterfly.

"Sha, I'm proud of you for staying sober. It must be – what...

about a year now?"

Wham! Out of nowhere.

I'm quiet as I decide whether to tell him, or save him from my confession. I don't want to disappoint him. Again.

Should I tell him, or leave him with that picture of me as being strong enough - good enough - disciplined enough. Am I saving myself, or him?

The flash in my cheeks gives me all the information I need. It's the same burn that I got as a child when I was caught. Embarrassed on one hand that I'd been busted. On the other hand, defiant with excuses.

"Well, Dad, I only have seven months. I drank right before I quit my job at the Pip-Tide."

I wonder how much disappointment he can manage in his current condition.

He looks at me, longer than is comfortable, but there is no information in his gaze. I shift my glance to his shoulder.

"Well, it sounds like you're doing fine now. I'm still proud of you." And his jaw is still.

I bend down again and give the kind of half-hug a hospital bed forces, my head against his chest. When I stand, a damp spot remains on the hills and valleys over his heart.

CHAPTER TWENTY-FIVE

Newport, Oregon

Through my support groups, I've heard about this guy, Rich Wisner. I've wanted to meet him because he's a captain on merchant vessels. I want to ask him about how to get my z-card so I can work on inspected vessels. Stable pay, safer boats.

I find him at a meeting in our recovery club. Nobody told me how good-looking he is. He has the most definite brow, nose and chin, each one sharp, detailed and angular. His face is some sort of alchemy between working man and royalty. His features, along with his nearly black hair, deep brown eyes and dark coloring, give him the look of an Indian prince. He's taller than me and, though I typically don't bother with such things, I guess he'd be especially attractive in tighter fitting blue jeans.

We're through with the formal part of the meeting where we sit around talking about how it is to be sober. Some people jet out the door, and though I'd like to join them, I hang around and visit. Today, I have a goal: Talk with this man about getting a z-card so I can work on better boats.

The club occupies the top floor of one of the rattiest commercial buildings in town. Even before starting up the stairs, the smells of burned coffee and nicotine whoosh down in greeting. They grow stronger with each step. The off-beige walls hold dents and nail bites from ghost art. Perhaps the rectangular shadows of color were once posters of meandering forest paths that lead to pinpricks of eternity. Fluorescent lighting offers an Elmer's glue-like coating to everything it touches. But, for those of us unlikely enough to make it into this hovel, it's a reprieve. For me, it's the place I find hope, and other people on the same road.

The room on the right, the one we've just left, is set up for formal meetings. The tables form a square with a space in the center. They're made of particle-board and covered with paper that's supposed to look like wood. It's peeling at the edges and swollen in places. The floor throughout the building is mottled beige — a color that's supposed to hide the dirt. It likely worked for the first forty years. A thin line of black surrounds each six-inch tile; decades of collected shoe jam and donut droppings. No amount of cleaning can take it away; nothing short of a match can fix it.

On the other side of the entry hall, there's another room. It's set up like an open living room and kitchen. Folding chairs are placed haphazardly, along with couches and easy chairs that a bunch of former drunks and their families were tired of. The kitchen's mismatched mugs and plates have the same origins. The regulars, like me, have our own glass mugs with our names etched into them. The 'in' crowd.

When we retire to the living room, Rich heads to the coffee pot, and I make my move.

Feeling like a teenager, I walk over and we get introductions out of the way.

I notice my arms are across my chest, grabbing each other for comfort. I unwrap them and force them to dangle to my sides.

"How long have you been sober?" I say to break the ice.

"A month. How about you?"

"It's been about a year for me."

Odd that I don't find it strange to start a conversation with such a personal question. Odd that he acts like it's perfectly normal.

There's an uncomfortable pause, and I'm afraid I'll lose him before I can ask what I came to ask. My arms begin their move back up toward my chest. They get about halfway when I stop and return them to dangle awkwardly from my shoulder sockets: Feigning relaxation, faking comfort.

"I'd like to get my z-card. I heard you have yours?" I turn my last sentence up with a question.

"Yeah, I've been shipping out for a long time."

"I want to get into the Merchant Marine, but I've heard it's a Catch-22. You need a z-card to get a job, and you need a job to get a z-card?" Another question that isn't. Embarrassed at my inability to be at ease, I shift my feet in an effort to expel energy. I catch myself, then stand still again as he answers.

"Well, yeah, in theory, but if you apply for a job, the boat can give you a letter, addressed to the Coast Guard, saying that you've got a job that's contingent on getting the card."

"Really? That doesn't seem so hard."

I relax, he's a nice guy, and he isn't bothered by my questions.

"Most people don't follow through," he replies.

"Thanks," then a pause. "Well... it's good to meet you. Hope I see you around." I'm reluctant to end it, but there's nothing else to say.

"Yeah, you too."

As I walk away, I feel like my life is about to change for the better. Like each breath that fills my lungs sends energy to each cell, from my crown to my little toe. No more Buddys.

While I'm thinking about my options, the captain of the fishing vessel Norske Sea calls, out of the blue, to say he's looking for a cook up in Dutch. I've never heard of the boat, and never heard of Captain Sterling Skor who carries his Norwegian accent like an elephant carries its trunk. It's not clear where he got my name and number, but apparently, he's desperate for a cook. As in tomorrow desperate. They're fishing for black cod on the Bering Sea. Other than helping on deck once in a while, I'd be the cook. I'd need to be on board in thirty-six hours, leaving less than twenty-four to make travel arrangements, find someone to sublet my place, say goodbye, and pack my bags for three months at sea. I say "yes."

CHAPTER TWENTY-SIX

Dutch Harbor, Alaska

The plane landing is manageable this time; I'm prepared for the cliffs of Mount Ballyhoo. I get an aisle seat and stare straight ahead. I gather my gear like a pro and catch a cab to the boat.

At 180 feet long, the Norske Sea has classically graceful lines but her white marine enamel is bleeding rust like a leper bleeds skin. I announce my presence before boarding, like I'd knock on a neighbor's door.

"Hello! Anyone aboard?"

A tall, thin man with that sandy colored hair that isn't really a color at all comes out, wiping his hands on a dirty, red engine towel.

"Welcome aboard. You must be new cook. My name Jordan."

His accent is even heavier than Sterling's, and every word is forced and clipped. But his relaxed attitude puts me at ease.

I put my hand out hesitantly. Jordan looks at his grease-filled hands, smiles, looks at me and shakes his head left to right and back. I smile back with gratitude as I throw my sea bag onto the deck from the dock. Seeing no ladder, I climb through an opening in the rail next to the bag.

Jordan leads the way into the house without a word. We walk along a short passageway past a door and another corridor, then enter directly to the mess deck where there's a man sitting at a table. He's reading from a stack of papers on a clipboard. His weight tells me that he's likely the captain, definitely not someone who packs much deck-work into a day. He's focused on the papers, but looks up and motions to the chair across from him. I sense right away that Sterling is a matter-of-fact kind of guy. Jordan exits back the way we'd come.

"We leave tomorrow. There are eleven of us. We're out until we run out of bait, or the hold fills with fish. I need food order in two hours." No wasted introductions here.

"Two hours?" I try to sound as normal as possible, but it's a good thing this guy doesn't know what's normal for me. I know I've heard him right, but I'm certain he can't mean it.

Instead of responding, Sterling gets up and starts to walk out of the mess room. He turns and looks at me as if I should follow, so I grab my bag and go after him. He stops at a door and opens it.

"Here's your room, you unpack later."

Deja fucking vu.

Food for eleven for an undetermined amount of time. The fresh food won't matter because most of it will run out in a couple of weeks. But two hours isn't long enough to put an order together, let alone take an inventory. I end up pulling numbers out of the air. One thing I know is that I'll need lots of flour to bake bread and desserts. I order 150 pounds. I split the meats into chicken, pork and beef. There's no fish on the list. It's crazy to order frozen when we're in the middle of the most productive fishing grounds on the planet. On the order sheet, I put a case of butter, four cases of eggs. Lettuce and spices, peaches and chocolate chips. And oatmeal, the perfect food. Breakfast or dessert.

In minutes under two hours, I have what, under normal circumstances, I'd call a rough draft. I'm not panicked because I figure I'll see the items I've missed as we cruise down the grocery store aisles.

Up on the bridge, I hand the order to Sterling. "Are you going shopping with me?"

"No, I go alone, he responds in his accent, "You stay. Make sure everything ready to take stores."

This doesn't sound right to me, but I'm tired and Sterling leaves before I can catch the words to use in response.

Later that day, the truck from the store drives down the dock with palettes of food. I stand on the deck with a copy of the invoice and a copy of my list, checking off items as they come aboard.

Case of green beans, check. Case of corn, check. Twenty pounds of flour. Odd. I make a slash on the left margin. Ten packages each of spaghetti, linguini and elbow macaroni, check. Brown sugar - five pounds. A quarter of what I'd requested. Butter. Same thing. Salt? Ten pounds. What the fuck? We have twice as much salt as we do brown sugar. I check the invoice against the original order. Sterling changed my numbers.

My skin crawls with a prickly heat, and I'm light-headed. Something like shame slides both up and down from my belly. Why had he even asked me to put an order together?

I finish taking stores on, but before they're put away I make my way back up to the wheelhouse.

"Captain, why did you change my order?"

"You order too much."

"Look, I bake bread every day, along with a dessert and cookies. This flour won't last a week."

"Too late to change now. Don't bake so much."

Is this the Norwegian stubbornness I've heard about my entire life?

I decide I'll make him understand the foolishness of his changes. I won't change the way I cook. I'll bake fresh bread and cookies until the flour, sugar or butter runs out. I mean, how much more could the flour possibly have cost?

Other than Sterling and Jordan, I'm the oldest person on board. I've always liked being the youngest, partly because I've known the rest of the crew has experience. The majority of this crew hails from the Midwest. Nebraska doesn't have a lot in common with Alaska, except the cold. It makes me nervous when I combine their origins with their age. But, there's Tommy, the Irishman. He's a Salt, for sure. North Sea, someone said.

On the water, my days are full. Again, I work through my seasickness, making sure there's always a toilet or bucket nearby. My deck work consists of baiting and coiling lines alongside my shipmates. We stand, assembly-line style, in the bowels of the ship, in front of boxes that hold short metal rounds that look like tire wheels. We grab the line and a hook, poke and slide a piece of squid onto it, coil, hang the baited hook onto the outside of the round, and move on to the next hook. Thousands a day.

Attached to buoys, the lines are set into the water where they drift, soaking in the ocean for up to a day while we set out another line. We return to the first line and haul it in with hydraulics, hopefully full of black cod. The fish are beheaded and frozen.

I'm baiting. How many thousands of squid have I poked a hook through? How many coils have I laid down? There is no counting. We've been at it for 24-hours straight and my body is a pincushion. I can't believe I'm capable of working so hard, for so long. Even unexpected sounds are painful. The deck boss, Eddie, appears next to me and I jump.

"You go on ahead," he says. "You can sleep for a few hours before you start cooking. We'll finish up here. Jordan will wake us when you've got breakfast ready."

I'm grateful, until I look into his eyes to give him my thanks.

I barely see the brown of his irises for the black of his pupils. I look at a couple of my other shipmates' eyes and, sure enough, their pupils are the same alien-orbs. I'm livid as I go to my quarters. They're on drugs; that's how they can keep these hours. They're putting all of our lives at risk. Worst of all, they never offered me any! I wouldn't have taken it, but that's not the point. They should have at least asked.

By the time I arrive in my quarters, I'm steaming. As I look into the mirror, I see that my own pupils are alarmingly large — in fact, as large as the guys'. They aren't on drugs — it's sleep deprivation. I fall into my bunk. Before I know it, Jordan is pounding on my door to start again.

CHAPTER TWENTY-SEVEN

Bering Sea

I'm beginning to get the picture that I'm a deckhand who also cooks. I spend about eight hours a day in the galley, so I guess that it is a cooking job. But, after that, I spend another ten to twelve hours below deck, baiting lines. Then we sleep for four or five hours, if we're lucky, and repeat. Today, it's my first sit-down after beginning work at 7:00 a.m., and it's midnight. Here I'd been, complaining about the menial job of cooking. I wanted to be a deckhand. This is what being a deckhand is.

I put out simple meals and snacks. Often times, I throw a roast in a pan in the oven and take a break later to add vegetables. Or I put together an old-time tuna casserole. Boil noodles, rinse. Put in a couple of pounds of canned tuna and a few large cans of cream of mushroom soup. Add a couple of bags of frozen peas and a spill of milk for consistency, then throw it in the oven with parmesan cheese and bread crumbs on top. It's almost impossible to overcook, and I can make it early in the day when I have one or two wits about me.

Sterling would have me spend even less time in the galley if he could. I draw my time out as much as I can by baking when I can get away with it, and by preparing breakfasts like bacon and eggs or casseroles instead of cereal or pancakes. But, to make my point, I still bake bread. I make cookies. Dammit, I'm going to run out of flour.

Sterling teaches me to prepare his version of salt cod. Take a large stockpot and fill the bottom with table salt. On top of that, layer cod filets, then cover it with more salt. Another layer of cod and on and on - salt, cod, salt, cod, until the pot is almost full. Cover it and let it sit for five days. When it's 'done,' rinse it off, add fresh water and potatoes, then boil the bejeesus out of it. But no amount of cooking is going to get rid of the taste of salt.

When we have the energy to converse and the engine isn't drowning us out, I learn about my shipmates. They're all from Nebraska and Iowa, never been to sea before. What the hell convinced Sterling to hire

139

a bunch of flatlanders to work the Bering Sea in the winter? One, maybe. But seven of them? He'd have to work to find so many green crew. It's frightening when I'm one of the most experienced aboard. But, we've got Tommy, and he's got an Irishman's knowledge of the sea.

Even with all the hours we're putting in, we're not doing so hot in the catching end, and now we're running out of bait. We head for St. Paul — the furthest populated island in the Pribilof group — to pick up more frozen squid.

We travel two days to learn that St. Paul has no bait. Sterling never thought to radio in advance for this information. To top it off, we're almost out of fresh food. We have cabbage and carrots left. I'm beginning to realize that my plan to run out of flour was not so bright. There's plenty of canned and frozen food, but something fresh – even bread or cookies – is always good for the spirit, especially when things are going wrong. And they are going really wrong.

With one day's bait left, we head back in the direction of Dutch Harbor to fish. There are no fish, so we turn around in fifteen-foot seas and run five hours, back away from Dutch, to use the bait we do have. By the time we arrive, it's too rough to fish, so we move and anchor for the day. Six days, wasted on one day of fishing, without catching a thing.

Next day, the weather improves, but the bait we have has gone bad, and below-deck smells like a rotted corpse. The guys throw cases of squid overboard. We'll have to return to Dutch to get more. It's a four-day trip with severe weather on the way.

We try to outrun the storm, but it's coming too fast. It overtakes us and hits us. Hard. There's no question of cooking. Even cold sandwiches are a challenge to put together. My usual strategy of waiting for a roll to open the refrigerator doesn't work. Things fly everywhere as soon as the door opens. I get fresh jars of condiments from storage to avoid the cooler. I stuff them between towels in the sink. But nobody comes to lunch. It's like a ghost ship, except for the sound of the engine.

Sterling's angry, I assume, at his run of bad luck. Personally, I consider it poor decision making. He runs the boat at full throttle. As we hit the tops of the waves, the propeller cavitates, catching air instead of water. While the prop is out, there is no control of the steering – not good when a 15' wave is beneath us.

Sleep is impossible. I lie in my bunk on my side, one knee shoved up against a bunk rail as tightly as I can manage, one foot and my butt plastering the bulkhead. My body is splayed out as far as I can reach to keep from being thrown out of bed. It's useless; I thud into the mattress after a second of near weightlessness. I have to get up. I collect all the pieces of me together, combine the coordination from my arms and legs with the strength of my mid-section to heave myself out of the bunk at exactly the right point of a wave, then stagger to the mess room, palms walking along the bulkheads, and legs outstretched to maintain balance.

The mess deck is empty, so I sit on a bench that's welded to the bulkhead. I spread my feet on the deck and my arms on the table. Out the porthole is an ever-changing view. From gray sky it jumps to the white tips of waves, then a solid wall of water. Within seconds, the ship is shoved upward and over to port. A mystery-can, maybe vegetables, has found freedom and is thwacking between the deck and bulkheads in the storeroom. I try to ignore it, but it's impossible. There is a moment of silence as the boat rolls to starboard. The can hits the bulkhead and stops for just a moment. The metal against wood noise is quiet, but as we begin to roll in the other direction, so does the can. It starts somewhat slowly, but within seconds, it picks up speed and rolls until the boat reaches the other side of the wave where it slams against the bulkhead and then begins its roll the other way. If I try to find it, I'll be thrown around, so I choose to put up with the sound that's as annoying as a dentist's drill.

I'm frightened. The crew's inexperience makes our situation perilous. They know the waves of wind on corn and wheat fields, not the power of water combined with a whole gale and no storm cellar. I love Iowans – my Mom grew up there. But Midwesterners are not who I'd choose to be around in an emergency at sea.

But there's Tommy. He knows what's happening. If Tommy isn't concerned, I needn't be.

Soon, however, Tommy comes onto the mess deck, swaying and bobbing like a drunken marionette. He looks at me and frowns in commiseration, then opens the door and heads up to the wheelhouse. Satisfied, I know he'll put sense into Sterling.

Relieved, I wait on the mess deck for the boat to slow down. A few minutes later, Tommy comes back down, his face white behind his weeks old beard. "I asked the Captain to slow 'er down and you'll not believe what he said to me," his thick brogue even harder to comprehend than usual. "He said 'She's like Humpty Dumpty - if she rolls over, she'll roll right back up again!'"

We look at each other for a moment, and Tommy disappears down the corridor to his quarters.

We ride out the next two days eating peanut butter & jelly sandwiches fortified with thawed out donuts that were left in the freezer from an earlier trip. In spite of Sterling, we make it into Dutch, but not before I decide I'm not going on another trip.

In port, after we've settled in, I head for the wheelhouse to talk with the captain before he has a chance to jump ship with the rest of the crew.

"I'm leaving," I say to Sterling in the calmest voice I know. "You'll have to find another cook." He looks at me, his eyes darken. I don't want to get into an argument, or even a conversation with him. I've said what I've come to say, so I turn and go back to my quarters to finish packing.

Legally, the ship is required to pay my fare home to Newport. I'm afraid to mention this to him. I'll deal with it when I get home. I can afford a plane ticket, but it will take every last ounce of money I have. I decide to walk the docks to try to hitch a ride. Maybe even find another job.

The weather is sunny and almost warm, but lots of boats are tied up because it's so sloppy at sea. Each boat seems to have a deckhand or two working on pots or nets. It shouldn't be too difficult to find someone heading south that I can catch a ride with.

I don't want my crewmates, and especially Sterling, to see me looking for work. I tell myself that if they see me ask for work and not get something, it will be humiliating. I hate having to ask to begin with. It's like I'm a failure all over again. Why can't I make one good decision? I move a few docks away and stop at the first occupied boat.

"Hey," I say to the man on deck. He turns his eyes to me, questioning with a slight tilt of his head. "I've left the Norske Sea. I need a ride south, and will cook in exchange."

He seems fidgety as he says, "No room aboard." He turns back to the net he's mending.

Surprised, not so much at the refusal but at his seeming lack of interest in me, I continue down the dock to the next, smaller boat. She's steel and looks like she's rigged for cod. I use a different approach. I put my hands familiarly against the rail of the boat in an attempt to appear like I belong. "Hi there. How's it going?" The deckhand looks up at me "Good." He returns to his work. This is not going as I planned. "I'm looking for work as a cook. I'm off the Norske Sea, and have references," not exactly sure what boat references I can muster.

"Don't need a cook."

They aren't impolite, but definitely do not want to talk. Boat after boat, I get the cold shoulder. Nobody wants to take a chance that I'll be trouble. As far as they're concerned, a young, single woman, alone in Dutch Harbor spells bad news. They likely think I'm gold digging. They avert their eyes, refusing to look at me once it's apparent I'm looking for work or a ride. Typically, guys in port are extra polite to me. But I've only known them in the bar, where they want something from me. Now, the tables are turned. I don't like it.

I end up paying for a ticket out of Dutch.

CHAPTER TWENTY-EIGHT

Newport, Oregon

Tired of life on fishing vessels – the long hours, the uncertainty of pay, I remember my conversation with Rich. I'm determined to find a real boat to work on, one with a sane crew and real safety equipment.

I hear about a job on the Research Vessel *Wecoma*. She's a 176-foot, steel ship. She travels to exotic places like the South Pacific. Warm places. Her homeport is my homeport, Newport. It's a galley-hand slot, but galley-hand on the Wecoma is better than cook on the Norske Sea. Pay by the hour instead of pay by the pound. Pay, period. Safety standards. Regular hours.

I apply for the position. I get the job. I get the z-card. Just like Rich said. Magic.

The Wecoma has a port cook who relieves the regular cook while the boat is in Newport. Jim is a retired chef, and a crew favorite. He knows what he's doing, and I'm disappointed that he won't be sailing with us. He has an easygoing, light-hearted way about him. I guess he's in his late sixties. His hair is silvery-white, and he has the nose of a hawk. His figure is evidence that he participates fully in testing the quality of each dish he creates.

Jim teaches me to cook simple things like quesadillas with shrimp. Two tortillas, one of them speckled heavily with jack cheese, dotted with cheddar. Diced green chilies sprinkled over that, then tiny pink bay-shrimp cover every round-inch in a single layer. The other tortilla tops it and a lightly oiled pan nestles and heats the treasure. Jim cooks it for two minutes, and then turns it gently to bask on the other side. Another minute to make sure the shrimp meat is warmed through, but still moist. He slides it onto the cutting board where I cut it into eight triangles. I slide the wedges onto the warming tray. Teamwork.

Jim teaches me, kindly and patiently, to make butter-cream icing. I learn that the butter needs to be cooler than room temperature, but not cold. I learn to whip the butter with a paddle on the mixer, and add the

145

absolutely-positively-sifted powdered sugar, to taste. A touch of vanilla extract, then he uses heavy cream instead of milk to soften the consistency. Drop by precious drop to soften, not liquefy, the confection. He teaches me to use the icing immediately rather than refrigerate it. Cold icing will not spread.

Icing my first cake is enlightening. I learn that there truly is a purpose for icing knives. Under Jim's supervision, I scoop plenty of frosting onto the center of the cake. Then, with care and tender words, I push it outward to the edges of the circle and allow it to avalanche down the side. I add more icing to the top center and repeat until every inch of cake is heavily covered in the delicate, off-white delight.

"Now what?" I ask of my mentor.

"I'll help you put the second layer on."

The cakes have been baked on oiled and flour-dusted parchment paper. With Jim's guidance, the second layer slides from the pan onto the top. I gently remove the paper.

I look to the master for my next steps.

"You can have a peaked cake or a smooth cake. Smooth is harder."

Wanting every bit of information I can get from him, along with any accolades he might part with, I respond, "Smooth."

"Okay. The top of the cake is first again. Use the knife to spread the icing, sliding along the surface at a 45° angle. When you've got it smooth, you can move to the sides, where you'll smooth again, but your motion should be upward, creating an edge along the rim. Remove excess icing as you go, but not too much. You want a nice, thick layer. You can scrape the knife along the edge of the icing bowl to clean it. Make sure there's no cake attached to it."

"Okay, but how thick is 'thick'?"

He touches his right thumb to forefinger and separates them to about an inch. "Like that. Maybe thicker."

I begin, tentatively, to work the top into a smoothish surface. I'm getting frustrated with how long it's taking. Even though it's clearly piled higher on one side of the top, I move to the cake's sides, thinking that the change of scenery might make it feel like I'm accomplishing more than smearing butter and sugar back and forth along the surface.

I'm working as delicately as I can, but a piece of chocolate cake breaks off, onto the knife. Without moving my head, and without breathing, I shift my eyes up to the top of their range and look at Jim, who's looking at me. He smiles the beneficent smile of one-who-knows, and walks over with a small bowl and indicates that I should scrape that piece of cake and icing into it. I do so and hand the spatula out to him but he refuses it. "This is your cake."

"Shit," I utter, expelling air through clenched teeth.

His expression makes it clear that he doesn't appreciate the foul mouth, almost as if the curse might have rolled off of my tongue and spilled onto the cake. But he continues. "You need to be more convincing when you push, otherwise the cake won't stay put. Scoop some fresh icing and place it on the platter, right below that crater you created."

Crater? That's an exaggeration. But I do as I'm told, and return my gaze to him for further instruction. "Now what?"

"Push it up the side, and then force it over your booboo. It should stick."

Booboo? This guy's a regular kick in the pants. But, I follow his directions and am rewarded. The icing adheres. I continue my scraping and smoothing, finishing the side. I then move to work the top again, pushing and smoothing the icing to the same edges that I'd pushed it up from. I'm going in circles in more ways than one.

I make no more booboos, but take more than an hour to get the smoothest finish I possibly can, but the icing is uneven and has blade marks clearly visible.

Jim inspects my work.

"Not bad for a first. I'll show you how to make it better, but I expect you'll learn to decorate without this later on."

I nod my acceptance of the future challenge.

"Grab a deep bowl and fill it with hot water, then grab a clean bar towel."

I comply and stand next to him as he dips the blade into the water and holds it there until the clinging icing melts. He removes it from the water and dries it off, then digs it, angled slightly, into the far edge of the top, drawing it toward him, removing a layer of the icing as he goes. He hands the knife to me.

"The reason you've put so much icing on the cake is so that you can remove it. Use the heated knife to skim icing until the top is flat. Then you can use the knife to melt out the lines."

I feel more like a novice carver, sculpting a masterpiece from cedar. My rounded top becomes flat. The butter melts beneath the touch of the warm knife, erasing the lines. I run the heated blade along the top, then the sides of the cake. Finally, Jim has me create a beveled edge all around, then make one last run along the side edge, then the top rim, to remove the rigid lines of the bevel.

My cake is close to beautiful.

CHAPTER TWENTY-NINE

Newport, Oregon

My only sister and I have always had a troubled relationship. With her birth came the threat of competition over the attention of my parents and brothers. She and I fought constantly. When we matured into young adults, we simply ignored one another.

But, when Margaret got pregnant, she must have been overflowing with hormones. She became pleasant, and I became pleasant right back. Pleasant ricocheted off of each of us until we turned nice. I shared her maternal instinct, though not her commitment. She became a mother, I became an auntie, we became friends. I already had a nephew, Patrick, and a niece, Nikoletta, both in NY, but I've only seen pictures of them. Miranda is a flesh and blood infant. I can gently sink my fingers into the baby fat of her arms and legs and that little baby butt of hers. I can hold her in my arms and inhale her baby scent – Johnson's with a hint of earwax and bellybutton lint. Do all babies smell like this? Musty and clean, like a pile of sphagnum moss after the fall's first rain. Miranda triggers the gene in me that wants to stay instead of go.

She's six months old when I leave for a seven-month trip to the waters around the Equator. Miranda will more than double her age in my absence. I'm having second thoughts – again – about this career of mine. How much will I miss her? How much will she grow?

I moved on board the *Wecoma* last night, and we left this morning. My art prints are taped to the bulkhead and a rug is thrown on the deck to cover the brown, indoor-outdoor carpet. My final personal touch is Bernard, the treatment bear. He's sitting, propped up against the pillow on my bunk. My room is as homey as I can make it. One of the guys laughed when he saw the throw rug. I can't imagine the response he'd have to Bernard.

The galley is different without Jim. Rodney joined us a few days ago. He's maybe 5'8" and 350 pounds. He owned a bakery, and is a friend of one of the regular crew. He seems nice enough, but I'm concerned about his size. I've never worked with someone so big. Working on a boat, even in the galley, is physically demanding, I wonder if he's up to it. I can't imagine him being light on his feet.

We pass through the jetties of Newport's Yaquina Bay and I'm getting a sense of the way this boat moves through the water. The perfect dance partner, she's in a waltz with the ocean, following every move without question, but keeping her balance at all times. It's almost like a fishing bobber might behave, moving in a circle, curtseying at each quadrant of the ship. She makes a pirouette, beginning at starboard forward. She circles and dips towards starboard aft, swoons to aft port, then ends and begins again at forward port. It's a slow dance since the ocean has lain down after a few October storms blew themselves out.

Still, I'm queasy within minutes of the first roll. Breakfast is, thankfully, done. I finish up the last few dishes and head for a lay-down in my bunk. As my head is level with Bernard's, the alarm shrieks. "This is a drill. All hands muster in the science lab. All hands to the science lab. This is a drill." I forgot about the emergency drill. Damn, Can't safety wait until I feel better?

I grab my survival suit and head for the ladder. Rodney's gotten there first. I can see immediately that his sea legs are even weaker than mine. He grabs for the rail with one hand and clutches his survival suit with his other. He yaws to starboard, his arm extending full length to hold his body barely upright. But he can't keep enough balance to lift one leg up to the next step. Even though the ladder on this boat is more like a staircase, Rodney can't navigate it. He steps down and, bowing his head, tells the line that's formed behind him to proceed. I feel my already quivering stomach sink in a sense of embarrassment for him, mixed with pity. It's not even rough out.

Moving past him, I mumble my thanks. I wonder whether his graciousness would extend to an actual emergency. I decide for sure I'll be wearing pajamas at night so I can get to the one ladder before he does.

Arriving in the science lab, Fred the Bos'n is standing along with the deck crew of Arnie, Alec and Bill. On the deck in front of them is a life ring attached to a rope.

When Rodney wobbles into the lab, Alec starts. "This is your emergency drill. Pay close attention because, if we do this again this trip," he pauses for effect. "It won't be a drill." The two scientists who were whispering stop and turn their full attention to Alec. I'm trying to concentrate, but am also measuring the steps to the back deck in case I have to use the toilet.

"First, we'll show you how to respond to a man overboard," he continues. I wonder how they do a man overboard drill. Isn't that dangerous? My oatmeal brain wonders which of us they'll choose. Damn, I'm miserable. Seasickness sucks, and I'd rather be dead. I look back to Alec.

Suddenly, the solution is clear. Me — pick me! Maybe the rescue will be unsuccessful. But Fred and Alec perform a mock retrieval, showing us to grab the rope rather than the buoy if we find ourselves in the water. Something about if we grab the buoy, the line will continue paying out, leaving us even further from the boat. I stop giving my attention because I couldn't care less about survival. I'm dying a slow death.

Then, Fred drags out Resusci-Andy, the mannequin.

"Now we'll have a real drill. This is Oscar," he says. "We're gonna to throw him into the water and rescue him."

"Oh, Gawd," I say out loud, my outgoing breath deflating my shoulders. Alec sends a brief, brotherly smirk my way. I squint my eyes and align my teeth in response.

The exercise goes off without a problem; Oscar is saved for yet another drill in the future. I return to my bunk and curl up like a snail.

Now that I'm an auntie, and was able to spend time with Miranda while I was in port, I'm sad to be gone. I admit I have some envy toward my sister. Maybe this whole family-love-motherhood-thing has merit. It's odd; there are people who envy me for my "adventurous life." If they only knew how boring living at sea can be at times.

Is it possible that the true adventure in life is persistence and continuity? Perhaps the challenge of loving another person is the truly daring deed. But, is there enough of me to give away to someone else? There isn't even a 'someone else' to give to.

Maybe I need to change my lifestyle – go back to school. Be

somebody – ha! But I know that's not what I want. What I want is my place, the spot where I belong. Not a physical space so much as a heart place. I want to know and be known. Not for my looks or my skills, but for me. It's odd that I'm so willing to put my body in jeopardy, but am terrified that someone might know my heart.

...and I don't think my 'place' means cruising around the world on whatever boat I can hitch a ride aboard. I'm tired of moving about with little to no connection to the people with whom I sail. Although camaraderie can grow between shipmates, I've never stayed aboard a boat long enough to build a relationship with someone. I wonder if I even could? Living on a boat isn't like living ashore. You can't go home at night. Every morning you wake up to the same people, day in and day out. They aren't family, and you didn't choose to be with them. Every night you sit down to dinner with people you didn't choose to be around. And if you don't like them, you can't leave. Every meal is one you didn't ask for, but there's no restaurant down the street where you can grab a burger.

All this forced interaction can make for limited engagement. People tend toward reluctance in opening up because, if you do get close to someone and they turn out not to be the person you thought, you can't escape them. It can get awkward. So, people generally stay at arms' length. Relationships are built more on work ethic and the ability to hold emotional boundaries.

Paradoxically, it can be like we're a family, arguing, playing around, and finding a genuine affection for each other.

And, if I'm going to be honest with myself, the boats have all chosen me. I've never said, "Hey, I think I'd like to work on that boat." I've been like the vellella velella, letting the wind carry me wherever she blows.

CHAPTER THIRTY

Tropical North Pacific Ocean

It's our third night out and my insides are dancing. Life is simple again. Is this my draw to the ocean? Every day a photocopy of the day before. All of my energies focused on creating food and cleaning up after food. I find freedom in the mundane. On the ocean, I have few choices to make. Everything is scheduled at the same time, every day. Wake, coffee. Read, meditate, write. Go to the galley. After work, thirty minutes on the exercycle in the winch room, shower, read, and bunk.

We're in the tropics. The closest I've been to these latitudes was as a child on spring break in Florida. The air is almost as wet as the water. The crew walks through the galley in slow motion, and I take my time emptying the trash out on deck, enjoying the breeze from the motion of the boat.

While a jet traverses a time zone in hours, we take days. Every three days, we gain one hour of time as we move west, toward the international dateline. When we hit the dateline at 180° of longitude, we'll jump ahead twenty-four hours and be in the following day, as in tomorrow. Time travel. Whoopie. There is, however, one damper: The crossing ceremony.

Mariners celebrate certain rites of passage, like land people celebrate First Communion or Quinceañera. They occur at a number of nautical points on the globe: Equator; dateline,;Arctic and Antarctic circles being a few of them. Alec comes into the galley to talk about my upcoming initiation into the Realm of the Golden Dragon. It's one of two ceremonies I'm supposed to be subjected to this trip. Rodney is also expected to participate, but Alec gets a thrill out of pre-torturing me.

He uses his best pirate accent, "So, are you ready for your initiation, Slimy Pollywog?" calling me by the name sailors are given before they're initiated. "Ready to become a Son of Neptune?" Then, he leaves the pirate behind. "Well, guys become Sons of Neptune. I guess that would make you a Daughter of Neptune."

"After that," the pirate continues, "You'll become a Slimy Pollywog again so you can become a Trusty Shellback at the Equator."

Back to his Alec voice again, he says, "That's the way it usually goes, but we're gonna be soft on you. Instead of having an initiation for the dateline and the equator, we're only gonna give you one."

"Why does this not excite me?" I reply.

"Look," he continues, almost in a negotiation, "Neptune has to give his permission for you to cross those lines, so we have to have at least one ceremony to ask his blessing. Besides, if you're going to be a mariner, you need to become a Trusty Shellback, which you can't do without Neptune's permission." Like he's talking about the rules of gravity.

"Oh." I say, in as bored a manner as I can muster. I'm tearing lettuce for the salad bar. He's got that teasing look about him. Alec has icy blue eyes that remind me of my dad's. They can be warm and welcoming. At times like this, playful shines out. There's laughter in there, mischievous laughter. I'm guessing there's also a fiery side of those gorgeous eyes.

I can tell that he wants me to ask more questions, but I'm not so sure I want to play along. I've learned that sometimes, the best way to fight back is not to fight at all. This has the feel of a quiet fight, maybe a pillow fight in a silent movie. He's baiting me by floating a feather in the air.

"Okay." I return to the lettuce, as if I don't care. The feather wafts to the deck without the slightest breeze.

He starts to walk away, but pauses and says, "Will you be there to watch the compass change?"

"What?" This is a new one, and he's tricked me into giving him my full attention.

"When we cross the dateline. You know, when the compass changes." As if everyone knows this fact and he's reminding me. "When east becomes west."

"Oh, come on. No way," I say.

"Yeah, it's true. How else could we get back to east?"

My mind searches through everything I know about longitude. I'm done in less than twenty seconds.

"I don't believe it," I say with a finality born of instinct rather than knowledge.

"Fine. That doesn't change the fact."

He has a bouncy saunter as he returns to his rounds, whistling. I continue to apply logic to the statement, but without knowledge, I'm lost.

Although I fight Alec about the crossing ceremony, inside I look forward to being an initiate. I smile inside at the prospect of saying, "I did it. I've arrived. I've made it through their test and now I'm one of them."

The closer we get to the dateline, the more animated Alec becomes about the crossing. He's also getting excited about this supposed compass switch.

"Hey, we're getting close to the dateline. I think it's going to happen on my watch, between 0800 and 1200 tomorrow. You'll be awake, are you going to come up to the bridge and watch?"

"Alec, you are so full of shit. The direction can't change like that. You're pulling my leg."

"Am not. It's a big deal, and not many people even know about it, let alone get to see it. You'll kick yourself if you don't."

"Give it up. I'm not biting."

"You don't believe me? Ask anyone. Ask Fred. He'll tell you. No, better yet, ask the Old Man. Let's go, right now. Put that knife down and we'll head up to the bridge and ask him."

"Fine." It's the kind of 'fine' that murmurs fuck-you under its breath.

I slip the knife under the cutting board to keep it from sliding and take my waist apron off, flinging it onto the counter. I follow Alec up the ladder to the bridge where Captain Doug is standing, looking at charts. I stand a few feet behind him, waiting to be recognized.

"Ask him." Alec goads.

The captain turns around and looks at me. "Did you have a question?"

"Alec says east turns to west when we get to the Dateline." It lunges out of me like a confession, or maybe a tattle.

"And?" he asks, as if I need to follow the ridiculous disclosure up with an explanation.

"I don't believe him." Firm. Knowing. I didn't know I could be so bold around him, but there it is.

"Well, you can come up and see, if you like."

"Th-thanks," I reply because I don't know what else to say. If the captain says it, it must be true. He's not the kidding type, Mr. Straight and Narrow, that's him. I don't think I've ever seen him crack a smile. Well, there was that once when he and the chief scientist were talking on the back deck. He laughed outright. I would have loved to have heard whatever it was they were talking about.

I set my alarm for 0500, an hour earlier than usual, in case we're ahead of schedule. I brush my teeth and hair, and then get dressed. I head directly up to the wheelhouse. The captain's there, but he's not on watch yet.

He turns, almost as if he's been expecting me.

"You missed it. If you'd been ten minutes earlier, you would have been here when we crossed."

"I got up early because you guys said it would happen between 0800 and noon." Whiny.

"Well, the thing is, we made better time last night than we thought we would."

"Oh," my outside voice says while my inside voice is screaming: Why the fuck didn't someone knock on my door? You get me all worked up over it, and then you completely ignore me when it happens. God, you guys are jerks. I'm deeply disappointed.

I make a sideways leer at the compass before I head back down to my quarters. It looks the same as it did yesterday, but then, I was confused to begin with.

A few hours later, Alec comes in for breakfast. I'm meticulously ignoring him, refolding the dishtowels and checking to make certain the oven is turned to the exact. right. temperature. He stands for maybe fifteen seconds at the imaginary line where my territory begins. "I heard we crossed early. That's tough luck."

"Someone could have told me."

"Yeah, well... maybe you can see it on the way back across. Look at the bright side — you still have the Equator crossing ceremony. And I need to talk to you about that. The galley's gotta get stuff ready for it. We need cooking oil. Plus we make a slime out of canned anchovies and ketchup." He looks down at the beige tiled deck, thinking. "Oh, and we collect the trash for a few days, then let it sit for about a week before the ceremony so it can get ripe. I'll take today's trash from you."

"Gross. What do you use it for?"

"Well, Arnie's agreed to be the Royal Baby. He smears the oil all over his big fat belly, and you kiss it."

"You are not getting me to go near Arnie's belly, especially unclothed. That's disgusting."

"Disgusting's the point. You'll eat the anchovy mix. After that, we throw the kitchen trash on the deck and you crawl through it. But we'll wash you down afterward with the fire hose."

"You're going to have to get that crap ready yourself. Even when you do, you're not going to have me as a player."

"It's the rule. No participation, no crossing certificate."

"What certificate?"

"Everyone who crosses the dateline, equator, or a polar circle gets a crossing certificate. That way, when you cross again, you can prove it so you don't need to go through it again. Then you get to watch other people go through it."

"If everyone gets one anyway, I guess I don't have to participate in your silly games."

"Nope. The Old Man won't give one out unless you've been through the ceremony."

I'm silent. I'm finding it hard to believe that the captain would be a part of this. My earlier excitement at being initiated flags.

Alec continues. "We haven't decided whether we'll shave your head. Personally, I think that's extreme."

Alec goes forward to look for his supplies. I tell myself that they can't force me to do that stuff. Still, I feel like I did when my brothers threatened to throw me in the muck-side of the lake.

We're nearing the equator. The weather is sultry, and it feels like the sky is closer; it's pressing the air into a smaller space. I feel heaviness bearing down on my skin, as if gravity has special privilege here. The tropics are like sex, hot and steamy in a way it's impossible to imagine when I'm not right in the middle of it. Days are in the nineties with the relative humidity at almost a hundred percent. When the sun goes down, a blanket of air reclines on top of me, weighing me down in an almost comfortable way. But, if it gets hotter, what is now soft summer cotton will become oppressively damp wool.

I go outside at night to take in the cooler air, and look up at the stars. There's an anchor winch on the forward deck that I use as a backrest while I sit, gazing into the night sky. I close my eyes, enjoying the slight breeze created by the movement of the ship. I take the air in through my nose as deeply as I can, then allow it to escape through my barely parted lips. I can feel the salt-tinged air on its way into my lungs. It coaxes my body to shift down, into neutral. The thrumming of the engine is a comfort in the background.

But when I open my eyes and look up, I experience a slight vertigo. I'm disoriented, certain that a strong breeze would toss me over. I'm almost dizzy when I look up at the freckled sky. Everything else is so pleasant, but I don't understand why the sky is so unnerving.

I hear his whistle first, then Alec's steps on the metal deck as he comes on his evening rounds.

"Oh, hello there. Enjoying the stars?"

I stand up so I'll be eye level with him. "It's beautiful. Reminds me of being a kid on the East Coast, except darker."

"Yeah, I love this part of the ocean - peaceful. How 'bout that Southern Cross?"

Of course! That must be why I'm disoriented. The Southern Cross has replaced the Big Dipper, and the entire sky is different than it is at home.

"Where is it?"

"Well, first you have to make sure you're not looking at the false Southern Cross. The true one is shaped like a cross. The false is more like a diamond, and sits higher in the sky right now."

He comes closer and points to a spot in the heavens. "Right there. That's the Southern Cross. Its stars are brighter, too."

"Where? I don't know where you're pointing."

He steps directly behind me and raises his arm over my shoulder. "Look right down to the tip of my finger and out." I smell shampoo. What is it, some grocery aisle brand? Citrus and earth.

After a minute of trying to match the angle of his pointer finger without spooning him, I have success, "I see it!"

"And right there is Alpha Centauri. That bright one, there." He moves his arm and finger down about an inch. "The sky's different here.

At first, looking up can be disorienting."

"I know what you mean. It's eerie."

"Yeah."

We stand, quietly looking at the stars for a few breaths.

"You know," he says quietly, "You don't have to shave your head. I was kidding. And we won't put that stuff on Arnie's belly. We're not gonna put you through that whole thing. No trash to crawl through."

What do you mean, no ceremony? How do I become part of the crew? I didn't want to roll around in trash or kiss that fat belly, but it was my "in," my way to be a part of, rather than apart from. My brain is battling, but I'm not willing to show it.

"I thought you were pulling my leg, but for awhile, I wasn't sure."

"Yeah, well it's our only entertainment out here."

"I can see that."

More silence as I consider the idea that there will be no formal entry into the club. I feel betrayed.

Alec looks down and shifts his feet, then off in the distance.

"And..." he begins.

"And what?"

"Well, you know the whole dateline crossing thing?"

"Uh, yeah?" My eyes squint and my tone rises up in a question.

"Well..."

I wait.

"That wasn't true," he says.

"You sonofabitch!"

Alec is laughing now, backing up. "You were tough to convince."

"You mean the Old Man actually lied to me?"

"I don't recall that he lied. More like he didn't tell you the truth."

"What a set-up! You guys were all in on it?"

He smiles.

The next morning at breakfast, I'm like the prom queen. Nick, usually taciturn, is smiling at me. Bruce laughs openly when he sees me and calls across the mess deck, "Hey, Alec! What's our heading?" Everyone laughs. I give a half smile and shake my head in mock disapproval. It's like I came home to my brothers stuffing my socks into the central vacuum system. I'm supposed to be mad, but the attention feeds my soul and gives me a connection and a sense that I belong. I've made it into the club. I'm one of the guys.

CHAPTER THIRTY-ONE

Tropical North Pacific Ocean

We motor southward. In our wake is a wash of phosphorescence. Tiny creatures spawn an eerie whitish-green in the water-world. Beneath the boat is a universe as brilliant as the one above; constellations of luminescence, a mirror of the sky. I stand at the stern, transfixed by this magical place where the fish fly onto the deck, the water glows, and the Southern Cross lives where the Big Dipper once weighted the sky.

I continue to go out on deck in the evenings to enjoy the stars. Like the Milky Way, Andromeda is an opaque blanket of white, fading here, growing stronger there. Some nights, it's like a dream, and I can see it only when I gaze lazily from the corner of my eye, as if I have to trick it into showing itself. Other nights it blazes across heaven. From time to time, meteors streak through the blackness.

It's during these times that I know, temporarily, the peace my father seemed to feel at sea. In this moment, there is no tomboy. There is no girl in a boy's world or woman in a man's. I live in awe with the warm breeze coursing over my skin. The monotony of thirty days at sea slips into the depths and there is only this one moment. This one constellation, this one sky. No need to prove even one thing.

During my afternoon break, I sunbathe on the forward deck. The ocean is calm and blue. We can see hundreds of feet down into the water, and the sea's temperature is 94° Fahrenheit. It'd be fun to dive off the side of the boat, but the rest of the crew says there are poisonous sea snakes. Maybe they're fibbing again, but I'm not interested in testing it.

Nights, it's too hot for the exercise bike, so I go directly to my room after my sunbath. Tonight, I find a plastic yellow rose, taped to my door. I stop in front of it, wondering why it's there. No note, only the rose, secured with black electrical tape. I begin to peel it off gently, as if it's made of leaves and petals rather than plastic and silk. I hold it in my hand, turning it, looking for a clue to the identity of person who gave it to me.

I'm startled by a voice. "Ralph," says Nick from behind me. He's talking about the chief engineer.

"Ralph gave me a rose? Why?"

"I dunno. Ask him."

I turn back to my door, twist the handle and step in, all the while looking at the rose. Ralph's always talking to me about his wife, so I know there's nothing other than friendliness involved. I put the rose on my desk and curl the bottom of the wire into a flattened circle so it stands upright. I never thought I'd see the day I'd prefer a plastic rose to a fresh. It will last as long as I do.

Next morning, I run into Ralph. "Hey! What's with the rose?"

"Who told you?"

"Nick."

"Well, it was supposed to be from Anonymous, but it's a make-up for the date-line thing."

I turn back to my work and smile.

I'm standing on deck as we motor into Honolulu. I almost swoon at the soft lines of the tropical island paradise. It's that time of day when the sky sighs, and her outward breath is a glow of warmth that covers the dusk in apricot. The ocean is her own name, Pacific, and even the soft breeze drowns in tranquility. I spend a few evenings on tropical beaches before I head home to stay with my brother, Bob, for a vacation.

CHAPTER THIRTY-TWO

Newport, Oregon

I go over to Dad's place to get his help with an oil change in my new-to-me car. I'm not looking for him to actually change the oil; all I want is backup in case I have a question in the middle of the mechanical operation. I've done it before, but not on this car. It's a used Honda Prelude. Black with a moon roof. It's the first nice car I've ever owned and the last thing I want to do is mess it up. More than that though, it's an excuse to be with Dad.

Dad and I have a 'do something' relationship rather than a cuddly one. The last time I remember being in his lap, I was about eight, maybe younger. In fact, that may have been the last time we intentionally touched. I've learned that if I want to spend time with him we go fishing or change the oil or shop for my mother's birthday gift. Our times together have goals.

I pull the car into their driveway. I've tried again and again to name the color of the house, but a single-word description eludes me. It was mixed at the recycle center from a bunch of leftover browns, tans and whites, with maybe a hint of mauve. Always thrifty, Dad got a good deal on it. Mom's thrifty, too, but she has good taste. I'm betting Dad won this color argument.

I enter the house yelling "Hello." He's right there, sitting at the kitchen table with a glass of iced tea, reading the newspaper. But it's a different table. Instead of the rugged wooden table he's sat at my entire life, he's at a round, glass-topped table that seems almost dainty.

He lifts his shiny eyes up so that he's peering over the rim of his reading glasses. "Hi Sha."

"Hey Poppolo. What's with the table?"

"The old one was too big for this place. There's just your mom and me, and we didn't need all that space."

I grab a chair and sit down, looking at the filigree. "Pretty."

Dad picks up his glass and drains the transparent brown liquid, slides his chair back from the table, and stands up. He's wearing what he always wears — brown coveralls. They have a diagonal pattern to them. Quite the fashion statement — herringbone coveralls. He always wears them because he always has a project going.

"Ready?"

"Ready. Car's out front. Just need you to guide me onto the ramps."

I stand again and we walk through the kitchen and laundry area to the two-car garage.

Dad's shop is full of the small tools he uses since he retired and became a putterer. Clamps and vise grips, drills, and an agate tumbler. Hand tools and power tools. Sanders, grinders and anything else he can get his hands on from the yard sales he and Mom ply. Everything is neatly organized on and around his wooden workbench that takes up one wall. Shelving lines another wall, leaving room for Mom's car. When it comes to garages and mechanics or carpentry, Dad is a perfectionist, but I never think of that before coming to get his help. I only think about spending time with him.

He pushes the button to open the automatic door as I move toward it. I fold at the waist and exit, get into the car and start it. He guides me onto the red metal ramps. He extends his arm, straight out, and gives direction by folding and straightening his fingers back and forth, palm up — like a one handed clap. When I get close to the edge he lifts his other arm to show decreasing distance with thumb and forefinger, then he makes a fist to let me know it's time to stop. A 747, safely landed.

I reach down and pull the hood release, turn the engine off, and get out. At the front of the Prelude, I reach out to complete the release of the hood, but he's quicker and opens it. He pulls up the metal stick that holds it open, and rests the hood on top of it. I grab a couple of wrenches off the workbench and bring them over. He's got the oil pan ready, and I slide under the car and loosen the oil pan plug, moving the pan beneath it. I slide a wrench onto the filter and snug it on, then move it counterclockwise to loosen the round, plastic filter. I'm feeling smug at my oil-change literacy as I slide myself back out from under the car while the oil drains. Dad's got the fresh filter sitting on the car's hood. I grab it and remove it from its cardboard box, then open a quart of Quaker State and dab a smidge on my finger to lubricate the gasket on the filter. At the same time, Dad nags at me, "Remember to put oil on the gasket, it'll make a better seal."

I slide back under the car to plug the oil pan and put the new filter on. Dad continues giving instructions, "Make it good and tight, but not too tight. But make sure the oil pan plug is in tight." Forgetting I'd been the one asking for help, I roll my eyes. I mean, am I not getting this all on my own? Why is he giving me these piddly-assed instructions — like I'm a child. Do I not know this shit already?

I return from underneath and drop the crescent wrench near the battery, harder than I ought. I want him to know I'm mad, but don't dare say I am.

I grab a few quarts of oil and, one by one, open and upend them into the engine.

He fusses, "You shouldn't leave that wrench there. You could close the hood on it."

I grab the wrench, bend down to pick up the filter wrench and return them to the workbench, building up steam.

"Let's look and make sure everything else is in good shape," he says as he moves beside me at the bench and reaches out for one of his metal tool cases. Out of it, he grabs one of those do-hickeys to test the battery fluid. He picks out an anti-freeze tester and takes them both over to the car.

"Dad, it's all fine. I just wanted to be sure I'm doing the oil change right. I did it right, huh?"

"Let's go ahead and check the other levels."

"Dad! The other levels are fine." I don't know anything of the sort, but now he has me pissed. I mean Christ — I ask for backup for the oil change, and he treats me like a complete idiot. I swore I wasn't going to get angry and here I am, pissed at him.

"I just want to know if the oil change is right!" The sting of a tear surfaces and I mentally shove it back.

Unheeding, he checks the other fluid levels. In order to ignore him, I check the oil dipstick and go to grab another quart to top it off. I come back to find him rechecking the oil I've already checked.

"You need more oil," he says.

Well, duh. Frustrated air flees my nostrils in a cross between a snort and a huff. But he continues through his checks as if he's heard nothing.

Wiping his hands on a beat up old terry cloth towel, he proclaims, "Everything else looks good, it's ready to go."

I walk away before he can begin the lecture on car maintenance.

Inside the house, I head down the hall to the bathroom to wash my hands. I hear the inside door to the garage open and close, then the kitchen sink water comes on. I close the lid of the toilet, then sit on it for a few minutes, gathering my breath. This movie is a repeat of every oil change we've done together since I bought my first car. I always forget that I get this frustrated with him, and I do it over. I don't remember how angry I get until I'm mad all over again.

I get up and go to the mirror and see my blotchy red face. I pat cold water on it in an attempt to shrink the blood vessels.

When I come back to the dining room, I'm less peeved, but still on edge. Dad's sitting down at the table, but his back is to it, and he's obviously been waiting for me. He says to me "Sha, turn around."

"Why?"

"You have something on the back of your shirt."

As I follow his direction, I again force air out through my nose, quietly this time. I gather my upper and lower lips between my teeth and squeeze the blood out of them.

"Come closer, I can't reach it."

Well why the hell don't you stand up and grab it? I shuffle back a step.

Instead of pulling the something off of my shirt, he grabs me clumsily around my waist and pulls me down into his lap.

I have no idea what's going on, but I follow his lead and sit.

Surrounded by him, I'm confused. The smells of his scalp and the engine-oil mingle with a hint of Old Spice. I want to stay mad, but it's as if this is what I've been waiting for. I'm thirty years old and I feel like I'm four and my dad loves me, just because I am. I melt.

We're still for a few seconds. I move one arm around his neck; both of his are around my waist, clasped at my left hip. I feel like I should put my head on his shoulder, but I'm too tall for that. We sit, father and daughter, neither of us comfortable, but neither of us wanting to give this moment up. That's because this is not one moment. It's a lifetime of missed moments.

"I love you, Sha."

"I love you, Dad. Thanks for helping with the oil change."

I get up, reluctant and relieved at once. I smudge my palm on my face, up from my chin, over my cheeks, using my pinky pad to push the tear out from my eye, across my temple. I tell him I'll see him later in the week and thanks again. Looking at him, I could swear his eyes are bluer than usual, glassier, maybe.

Two days later, he's gone. He's sixty-one. I think he didn't go fishing enough.

CHAPTER THIRTY-THREE

Eastern Pacific Ocean

Misty. The perfect boat.

Two steps up, grab the stainless steel railing, step onto the deck, and move out of the way for the next person. We six kids and Mom and Dad. Except Dad's in a cardboard box that wouldn't stand up to an October rain.

All of us together for the first time in a long time to say goodbye — to throw the scraps of his body into the sea. Memories fly by, but none settle. Bourbon, Old Spice and White Owl New Yorkers. Thumb between two fingers — gotchyer nose.

We cruise out to Yaquina Head. Perfect place for rockfish. But the fishing poles are all secured. We're here to leave something, not take it away. We make jokes and talk about everything except what we're here for, but that cardboard box is there on the galley table.

The engine shifts down a notch, then slows to a complete stop, signaling our arrival. We walk out onto the back deck and circle up in our life-long configuration – oldest to youngest.

Bob holds the box while Mike's opens it. He untwists the tie from around the neck of the heavy-duty, clear plastic bag. Mike opens the bag and grabs a handful of gray. He steps to the transom and, knuckles up, opens his hand and releases them.

Bob and Pat each make the journey in and out of the bag. My turn. I reach my hand in and pull a fist full of ashes out.

It's gray stuff. Lumpy gray stuff. But this particular gray stuff is my father. Here is the man who was so large, who sat me on his foot for rides and tucked me into tires and rolled me down hills. The man who had, in turn, both thrilled and terrified me, is sitting in a plastic bag, in my hands, on a boat, on the ocean. There should be more of them. More of him.

I clench the handful of ashes and small chunks of bone then move my balled up fist to the outside of the boat. I open my hand, palm up, to reveal the powder. I'm unwilling to let go, but a faint breeze comes by and takes the lighter ash away. Emboldened, I tip my hand, letting the remainder of Dad drop into the sea. The bone plops and sinks immediately into the depths while the ash floats, leaving a widening trail along the smooth, black surface. The trail becomes wider and more tenuous as it disperses out into the vast expanse of the Pacific. My hand closes, the inside encased in a faint husk.

I imagine him as he circulates and pools in the ocean. He runs up the creeks in the bellies of the salmon who spawn and die, releasing him to flow, back to the sea. The water evaporates and freezes and falls to the earth as rain and hail and sleet and snow. I imagine him, following me everywhere I go because water flows like veins in our world. Dad is in there, traveling the globe on the tides and currents, in the streams and rivers.

As he drifts away, I have a one-sided conversation with him. Maybe it's a prayer.

I'm watching your ashes — you — being swept away, into the tides and currents. Soon, I won't be able to tell you from the water, you'll be a part of it. I know I can find you there in the ocean, lakes, the rivers and streams. The rain and fog and the crust on top of a lake on a winter's day. The ocean and mud puddles. Ice, water and steam; liquid, solid, gas.

Tears flow down my cheeks. Dad's gift to me. Salt water.

Reviews are solid gold for authors; Please consider leaving one. Reviews anywhere are appreciated, but those on Amazon and Goodreads are especially valuable. Even if you didn't purchase your book through Amazon, you can still review there. Thank you so much.

Theresa Wisner is a US Merchant Mariner. She lives with her husband and German shepherd in Oregon's Coast Range.